Building Bricks
Without Straw

Dr. Bettye J. Alston

(Photograph by Larry Walker)

Building Bricks Without Straw

by

Dr. Bettye J. Alston
Memphis, Tennessee

FOUR-G Publishers, Inc.

2002

ISBN: 1885066-15-5

For copies of the book and inquiries,
contact:

Dr. Bettye J. Alston
Inside & Out Wellness Center
1024 S. Cooper Street
Memphis, TN 38104
TEL: 901-278-2112
FAX: 901-278-7306

Published by
FOUR-G Publishers, Inc.
P. O. Box 17035, 1400 Lynch Street
Jackson, MS 39217

Cover Design by Larry Walker
Illustrations by Donna Burnetti

Printed in the UNITED STATES OF AMERICA

CONTENTS

DEDICATION

This book is dedicated to the one and only, the most wonderful man in the world, my husband, Rev. Dr. Neasbie Alston. He is my pastor, my mentor, my friend, and my personal counselor. I love to hear him preach and pray. He is one of the most gifted orators I have ever known. When he speaks, I listen!

Life has been such a joy with him by my side. When I asked him to share in the writing of this book by contributing devotional readings for busy people, his immediate response was his usual one to my requests: "Honey, I will." His only questions were "How many?" and "When do you want them?"

We dress alike, we pray together, and we go almost everywhere together. Our favorite saying is; "When you send for one, you will always get two." Rarely are we seen apart.

My husband constantly assured me throughout the long months of writing this book that I would complete it on schedule and that it would be a blessing to those who read it. I know that whether it is a great success or not my husband will say that it is. He is just that kind of a guy.

Somehow, even though he had to clean the house, cook for himself, wash the dishes, run errands, and make sure that the house ran smoothly, my husband supported me, encouraged me to be all that I could be, and never once complained about the time I devoted to writing this book and working my business. He is one in a million, and I am so happy that he married me.

Our marriage has been a blessing to the both of us and has united our families into eight children, eighteen grandchildren, eight great-grandchildren, and many other extended family members. Friday, November 29, 1980, will always be in my memory. It was the day I had one of the largest, most grandiose weddings that has ever been held in Memphis, Tennessee, and it was the day I married the greatest man in the world.

ACKNOWLEDGMENTS

I must first give honor to God for redirecting my life and giving me a new purpose and mission that has broadened my ministry and provided me with an awesome challenge. If I had not known for a certainty that God called me from my many activities and caused me to focus on the single and very important mission of establishing wellness centers within local congregations, most likely I would have continued in image building and personal wardrobe enhancement. I should have known that I was going to finally write this book.

It appears that God has enjoyed having me to do each thing in my life that I declared impossible. No amount of protest, such as, "I don't have time" (I had promised never to read another book or write another paper after graduating from the university), could release me from the overwhelming belief that God wanted me to put aside everything I was doing and complete this book. To God be the glory. A new ministry has been started, and a once-thought impossible book has been completed.

Secondly, to my husband, Rev. Dr. Neasbie Alston, who has been the "wind beneath my wings" for twenty-one years, I thank you for becoming a house husband and doing everything for yourself in order to allow me uninterrupted times to write. Also, thank you for trusting me after your stroke and believing that I was competent and knowledgeable enough to help you regain your health and vitality through the use of my First Fitness products. As a result, God has blessed you to be symptom-free of diabetes and high cholesterol and to be physically fit again. It is a miracle to watch you each morning as you do three hundred, and sometimes four hundred, push-ups. That's not bad for a man approaching eighty years old, especially after having experienced that very debilitating stroke only two years ago. You are the greatest, and I love you.

I must acknowledge all of the friends and relatives, including Cathy Maxwell and Dr. Peggy Richardson, who helped to keep me focused and on track by constantly inquiring about when I would be finished writing this book. Each one of you should take credit for its completion because I would not have met my deadline for publication without your repeated inquiries. You kept me inspired to finish, and I thank you for your faith in me.

A very special thanks to my God-given daughter, friend, and confidant, Minister Jacqueline Pryer, for serving as my private secretary, typing for long hours, answering the office telephone, and keeping things moving while I "locked up" in my office to write. I can never thank you enough for your godly love and the help you have given.

To Larry Walker, for designing the book cover, and to my daughter Donna Burnetti for the sketches and graphics that appear before each chapter, thank you.

To Minister Jacqueline Pryer, Latonya Allen, Carol Chapple, and others who typed and edited my awful hand writing as I scribbled on anything I could find and gave it to them to transform into a legible, coherent, meaningful book, please accept my deepest gratitude. I know that your efforts were a true labor of love.

To my friends, Rev. Delores Currie and Shelley Baur, who shared with me, prayed with me, and loved me in spite of my not having much time to chat, due to the time required to write this book, thanks for understanding and being my friends.

To my church, New Beginning Ministries Church of Our Lord and Saviour Jesus Christ, thank you for the sabbatical you gave to me to write this book and live my dream. God bless you.

To my incredible team, *The Miracle Workers*," I appreciate the love, loyalty, and support you have shown me. I could not have completed this book without "the madness" we have shared. Each of you has a special place in my heart. I have learned so much from you and watched you wear the name of *The Miracle Workers* with pride and commitment. You are truly "Eagles." I have taught you well. Spread your wings and fly.

To Rev. Jini Kilgore Ross, who edited and assisted with the publication of this book, you are priceless. I could not have successfully completed it without your professional expertise. Your comments were welcomed.

Last, but not least, to my First Fitness family—Lee Causey, Nigel Branson, Eileen and Taylor Hegan, Billy and Eltha Banks, Gailey Ward, Pastors Andrea and Michael Dudley, and all of you that believed in me, as well as those who prayed for the success of this book, I thank you. I am privileged to have each of you in my life.

FOREWORD

Dr. Bettye Alston is one of the most powerful, brilliant, and driven women I have ever met. Upon first meeting her, I was immediately impressed with her openness, honesty, and purpose in life.

In this wonderful, inspirational book—without fear and without reservation—she takes you through her failures, trials, and tribulations to the incredible success she has achieved in her life.

She understands that the game of life cannot be played without the belief and knowledge of spiritual law. She knows the Old and New Testaments give the rules of the game with wonderful clarity. Jesus Christ taught that it is a great game of giving and receiving, and believe me, I have first hand knowledge of the incredible giving of Dr. Bettye Alston and her extraordinary husband, Reverend Neasbie Alston. They are the perfect examples of "whatsoever a man soweth that shall he also reap."

Someone once said, "There is a place that you are to fill, and no one else can fill it; a purpose you are to do, which no one else can do." Dr. Alston successfully and powerfully demonstrates how we all have a true destiny in life and how we should each remain true to that destiny. "Keep thy heart with all diligence; for out of it are the issues of life" (Proverbs 4:23).

Building Bricks Without Straw is a complete, integrated, Bible-centered approach to releasing the awesome potential trapped within each of us. With penetrating insights and spiritual anecdotes, this book reveals a step-by-step pathway to releasing your potential. If you have been frustrated by your dreams, ideas, and visions, this book will activate your buried treasure and ignite the wheels of productivity. It will release a crushing blow to uncertainty and procrastination. It will set you on the path of purpose to personal fulfillment, productivity, and ultimate success.

You will now be able to take the next positive step in your life to activate, stimulate, and release the wealth of your potential; to break free and leap the limitations and disappointments of the past and achieve and receive all the financial rewards and spiritual blessings that God truly wants for you.

Lee Causey, Founder
First Fitness, International

PREFACE

The provocative, dynamic, self revealing, refreshing, and inspirational thoughts in this book are designed to offer a new vision of biblical support and hope to the reader who is struggling to make a radical, life changing decision that requires him or her to perform a task that appears impossible.

Even though the book appears at first glance to be a how-to book for persons in network marketing, it is much more than that. It is an indispensable tool to re-vitalize faith and trust in God to always guide, love, and be there for Christians in need of divine intervention in order to achieve success.

It is my hope that readers will have the ability to remember a time when they really needed God's help, and God turned the would-be disaster into a triumph. Without complete dependency and confidence in the power of God to fight the battle, work a miracle when it is needed, or open doors that have been closed to us, each one of us would be laboring in our own strength and depending upon our own skills and power.

This book reveals the divine nature of God in relationship to the trusting Christian. The Bible, God's Holy Word, demonstrates and validates that we do not have to build bricks without straw. Rather, we are to seek God and depend upon His wisdom and inexhaustible resources to help us fulfill our life's goals, purposes, and missions.

With God we can accomplish anything.

Dr. Bettye J. Alston

INTRODUCTION

Once in a while we are privileged to meet an ordinary person with extraordinary countenance. Such a person is my friend and colleague, Dr. Bettye Alston. At first glance, she is simply an overachiever who is smarter than most and able to seize the moment. But on closer observation, her unique virtues—persistence, laser focus, ability to take rejection or disappointment while out-performing all competitors and still land on her feet—seem to fly out at you to capture your attention.

In her early twenties, she had found herself to be a single mother of four rambunctious children, so for that alone, I commend her. Not willing to settle for just supporting her family, she kept returning to school for more and more training, more and more degrees.

It couldn't have been easy. I am firmly convinced that Dr. Bettye Alston is who she is today because life did not always treat her kindly. She has learned to not only go with what she knows, but more importantly, she has learned the value of mentorship and masterminding.

If two heads are indeed better than one, then adding a few more heads to the project has got to be even more enhancing. Dr. Alston will do whatever it takes to absorb the knowledge and experience of the great minds that are out there. And she is timeless in her pursuit of excellence.

As an industry leader, what I have especially admired in Dr. Alston is her frequent recognition of her team members with gifts, flowers, and praise. I often think of how blessed we are to have this example before us. Dr. Alston truly ignites a spirit of teamwork in her walk with God, as well as in her walk with the Miracle Workers, exemplifying our scriptural observation of the importance of team unity: "If a house is divided against itself, that house cannot stand" (Mark 3:25).

And it would be remiss of me not to mention to you that Dr. Alston's husband, Reverend Neasbie Alston, is one of the finest human beings the world has ever seen, so I am sure his positive, wonderful energy will add a special blessing to you as well when you study his daily devotions contained within this book.

Life is full of choices. You made a choice to cross paths with the Alstons. Now you can make yet another choice to study this material and see what insights are contained within. I encourage you to enjoy this journey, to pray about the lessons you find here, and to use this platform to trigger the design of your life's purpose.

When you follow Dr. Alston's role model by living your life on purpose and being responsive to the lessons God has put in your path, you will be richly blessed indeed, for it would be a sad thing to have the experience without learning the lessons. I encourage you to glean new inspiration and hope from within these pages, and to go forth from this day forward, determined to make a positive difference in the lives of your loved ones and all those whose lives you touch.

Eileen Silva
Author, trainer, and metabolic
weight control specialist

My Story

Registered Nurse
Pastor
Wife
Mother / Grandmother
Great Grandmother
Counselor
Network Marketer?

Strong
Woman of God

Facing Destiny Very Afraid

Chapter 1

My Story

(Facing Destiny Very Afraid)

It was in the middle of what appeared to be a typical but hot, mucky, southern summer night at the end of August 1999, that I received the telephone call that ultimately changed my life! The call gave me a paradigm shift and thrust me into a new career. This new career was a scary, but secretly, long awaited, exciting adventure for me, a sixty-one-year-old grandmother and retiree.

Thirty-six years of registered nursing had been sprinkled with various pursuits. I liked being an image builder and personal wardrobe consultant for many outstanding women in my hometown, of Memphis, Tennessee. In addition, I had re-entered academic life fifteen years earlier as a single parent with four small girls and somehow succeeded in accomplishing the task of earning a masters degree in divinity. A few years later I earned a doctorate of ministry degree.

While at the height of my career as a registered nurse, God called me into the ministry in the African Methodist Episcopal Church and very quickly elevated me to the role of pastor. I was sent to a dying congregation and a dilapidated church in a very poor, impoverished section of the Memphis inner city. My primary task was rebuilding the congregation and restoring the church, which was in deplorable condition. Due to the church's condition, it was slated to be closed. The work was exciting, but grueling and required most of my waking hours. Twenty-four hours in the day were not sufficient for me to sleep, work, pastor the church, and spend quality time with my husband, Rev. Neasbie Alston, who was and is currently a minister and the pastor of a prominent Baptist Church located nearby.

Without a doubt, many of my friends thought that I had lost my mind when I enrolled in school again, this time to earn a Ph.D. After completing the requirements and earning the Ph.D., I was sure I had finally fulfilled what God wanted me to do. As a result, I would be able to relax, work in my dress shop, preach, pastor, go shopping as often as I wanted to, enjoy my grandchildren and great-grandchildren, and travel around the world with my wonderful husband.

Additionally, I planned to continue using my Ph.D. in counseling psychology, to counsel as time permitted. I knew that after retirement, my community and sorority involvement would also be expected to increase. Hopefully, I would also find more time to meditate, read my Bible, and swim in the backyard pool that my husband and I had built seven years prior. As yet, I had only managed to swim one summer holiday each year. My family felt as though I never had enough time to do anything but work. So my plans were made. I was going to get my life in order and do all the things I really wanted to do.

Without warning, my plans changed when I received a telephone call from Los Angeles, California. Not only was the course of my life changed, but also all of my personal plans suddenly became null and void. Gailey Ward, the caller, talked to me about a phenomenal and life-changing metabolic reset program called Suddenly Slim. She related to me how she used the program's products to successfully change from a size sixteen dress to a size twelve in just ten days. Her testimony sounded unbelievable. Being a size sixteen myself and desperate to lose weight, I asked her to come to Memphis for a visit. I needed to see her for myself. I could not believe she was healthy.

At my request, Gailey immediately purchased her ticket, and in two days she was standing at my door. She appeared to be very healthy and happy. Little did I know this impromptu visit by a total stranger would be God's method of starting me on another exciting segment of my life's journey. Without realizing it at the time, God was calling me to do something that appeared to be as difficult as building bricks without straw.

During my years as a Christian I have learned five things that God will do:

Teach us
Test us

3

Bless us
Lead and guide us
Be faithful to us

God is always faithful to do all of these things. God is the maker of miracles, and He loves to surprise us with winning results when things appear impossible. In the Bible we can read how God was faithful to Abram, Moses, Joshua, David, Jeremiah, Paul, and other great prophets, kings, messengers, and disciples that trusted Him. Therefore, I knew that He would also be faithful to me. As I endeavored to do something I had not done before, I put my trust in Him.

When God called Abram (Abraham), God told him to leave his kindred and country and go to an unfamiliar land; but God said He would be with Abram. So Abram left everything behind and started out with his immediate family, his possessions, and a promise from God. Abram was not told God's complete plan for him. He probably would not have believed if God had told him he would leave his home, pass through Canaan, and then later return to Canaan with his descendants in numbers unimaginable. I am sure the only reason Abram was able to believe God and do as God instructed was because he didn't know too much. In order to build bricks without straw the person must first be able to believe God. He or she must believe that God is able and can and will make the way that seems impossible, possible.

When we see in the natural, as carnal human beings, things will often overwhelm us. It will appear as if it would take a miracle to accomplish our tasks, but God makes the tasks simple and easy. God is the miracle maker, and we can become His miracle workers if we will only choose to allow Him to use us. Without Him mere challenges would appear insurmountable. But when God is in control, things that appear as large as mountains are reduced to the size of a grain of sand.

Moses and Joshua had many occasions to request and believe that God would work miracles through them as they sought to accomplish His will and purpose in their lives and the lives of God's people, the Israelites. Each man was placed in a precarious leadership position when God chose him to lead and to guide people who had their own ideas about the direction they should take and how they should live.

Moses has always been my role model, as well as my Godly inspiration. God not only divinely changed the direction of Moses' life and placed him in a leadership position he never expected to be in, but He also chose Moses to be His spokesperson before Pharaoh for the entire tribe of Israel.

While Moses was attempting to fulfill his assignment (which already appeared to be impossible), Pharaoh ordered the Israelites to perform the unheard of task of building bricks without straw (Exodus 5). The Israelites cried to Moses. Moses returned to God and told Him what Pharaoh had commanded the Israelites to do. God worked miracles through Moses and delivered His people from Egypt, so they never had to attempt to perform the difficult task.

Building bricks without straw is difficult enough, but surely if the Israelites had felt they were capable and experienced in doing so, they would not have feared performing the task. Prior experience would have provided them with confidence. Instead, Moses was the leader of people who had not previously had to build bricks without straw. And they certainly did not wish to perform labor under the conditions and deadlines they were given.

The call and subsequent visit that I received from Gailey Ward resulted in my undertaking the seemingly impossible task of building a business and network marketing team from a group of faithful, trusting friends and loyal acquaintances. The friends and acquaintances had little or no knowledge about network marketing. They had no prior knowledge of the business, products, or company I asked them to join. Even though I was not exactly a novice (due to having experienced three failed attempts to get network marketing teams built in other companies), I was definitely not the one to brag about knowing what to do nor how to do it. To make bad matters worse, I was somewhere between being labeled a crazy woman who does not know what she really wants to do and being on the verge of changing a lifelong career, and feeling euphoric about it. I felt as if I was standing on a ledge ready to leap into one of the most exciting adventures that I had ever experienced.

The excitement of the possibility of losing a lot of weight quickly, coupled with the opportunity to make millions in residual dollars greatly interested and intrigued me. I was propelled into a company that I would later come to realize as being my destiny and ultimate vehicle to success.

With fervor, I plunged into my task of building a team. I gave no thought as to how I would build a team or how I would actually work the business. I just knew it felt right and the time was now or never. I trusted that God was leading me into another phase of my life and that everything would work for my good.

Introducing my newly acquired weight loss and diet products to people who were already skeptical or afraid of them was truly a challenge since there had been a recent widespread scare over a prescription drug that reportedly had caused many health problems for people all over America. However, feeling excited, adventurous, and sure that I could do it (against the advice of many friends), I formed *The Miracle Workers Team* in August 1999.

With dollar signs in my eyes and a mental picture of the slender body I would eventually have, I was ready to work and soon was on my way to immediate, inescapable, wealth and health (or so I thought). Anyway, I was ready to face my destiny unafraid.

Ten Lessons To Be Learned from Chapter 1:

1. God is faithful—Trust Him! He works miracles when we need them. He is a covenant keeper.

"And they that know thy name will put their trust in thee: for thou, Lord, hast not forsaken them that seek thee" (Psalm 9:10).

"He hath remembered his covenant for ever, the word which he commanded to a thousand generations. . . . And he brought forth his people with joy, and his chosen with gladness: and gave them the lands of the heathen: and they inherited the labour of the people; that they might observe his statutes, and keep his laws. Praise ye the Lord" (Psalm 105:8, 43-45).
Please read Psalm 105:8-45.

2. Few people are already educated in the "how to's" of a new venture. The professional must take the time to learn just like other new recruits.

"And if a man also strive for masteries, yet is he not crowned, except he strive lawfully" (2 Timothy 2:5).

3. Do not depend solely on support from friends and family when starting a new venture. Their help may not come until later. Jesus said,

"A prophet is not without honor save in his own country . . . ." (Matthew 13:57).

4. Forget past failures, but learn from them in order not to repeat the same mistakes. Start each new venture afresh. Your greatest failure may occur just before your greatest success. "If at first you don't

succeed, try and try again."

"Brethren, I count not myself to have apprehended: but this one thing I do, forgetting those things which are behind, and reaching forth unto those things which are before, I press toward the mark for the prize of the high calling of God in Christ Jesus" (Philippians 3:13-14).

5. Do not try to buy your way to the top in network marketing. If you do, you will be sorry. The business is called network marketing or multilevel marketing for a reason. If you are wise, you will build a strong team and sell your products or service in order to properly maintain your position and / or move to the next level, or service in order to properly maintain your position and /or move to the next level.

"My son, attend unto my wisdom, and bow thine ear to my understanding: that thou mayest regard discretion, and that thy lips may keep knowledge" (Proverbs 5:1-2).

"Trust in the Lord, and do good; so shalt thou dwell in the land, and verily thou shalt be fed. Delight thyself also in the Lord; and he shall give thee the desires of thine heart. Commit thy way unto the Lord; trust also in him; and he shall bring it to pass" (Psalm 37: 3-5).

"Except the Lord build the house, they labor in vain that build it . . ." (Psalm 127:1).

6. Never try to manage your downline. Uplines get very upset when members of their downline will not work the business. Provide leadership support and assistance to those who request it and who show some interest.

"Counsel in the heart of man is like deep water; but a man of understanding will draw it out" (Proverbs 20:5).

7. Jesus was the first network marketer. He recruited twelve first line disciples, but he ended up with only eleven. Now his disciples have grown into the millions, and the gospel has been spread throughout most of the world. Remember, success is not assured by recruiting the many, but rather by the work of the faithful, passionate, and committed few.

"And the Lord said unto Gideon, The people that are with thee are too many for me to give the Midianites into their hands, lest Israel vaunt themselves against me, saying, Mine own hand saved me" (Judges 7:2).

"And the Lord said unto Gideon, By the three hundred men that lapped will I save you, and deliver the Midianites into thine hand: and let all the other people go every man unto his place" (Judges 7:7).
Please read Judges 7: 1-8.

8. We are never too old to learn something new. Do not fear reaching for the moon; if you miss it, surely you will at least reach the stars. Be adventurous!

"God hath not given us the spirit of fear; but of power, and of love, and of a sound mind" (2 Timothy 1:7).

9. Even though we make a foolish mistake, God is there to rescue us when we pray, repent, and ask for His help.

"O God, thou knoweth my foolishness, and my sins are not hid from thee. . . . Deliver me out of the mire, and let me not sink: let me be delivered from them that hate me, and out of the deep waters. . . . And hide not thy face from thy servant; for I am in trouble: hear me speedily" (Psalm 69:5, 14, 17).

10. God has a perfect plan for everyone's life. Once the plan is realized, purpose and mission will follow. Do not allow others to influence you to the extent that you do not heed and follow the plan God has for your life.

"And Moses called unto Joshua, and said unto him in the sight of all Israel, Be strong and of a good courage: for thou must go with this people unto the land which the Lord hath sworn unto their fathers to give them; and thou shalt cause them to inherit it. And the Lord, he it is that doth go before thee, he will be with thee, he will not fail thee, neither forsake thee: fear not, neither be dismayed" (Deuteronomy 31:7-8).

Looking Through
Rose Colored Glasses

Chapter 2

Looking Through Rose Colored Glasses

(Failing Forward)

My excitement and determination to build a very large, productive, network marketing team from loyal friends and family was very short lived. It only took the discouragement of some of my closet friends and a negative comment from my sister, Ruby Claxton, to cause me to doubt whether or not God really called me to do network marketing. Suddenly I was asking myself, "Who will be my clients?" "How will I market my products?" "Why am I doing this?" "What will people say if I fail?" These and many other questions rushed through my mind as I attempted to talk myself out of the venture I had been so excited about. Within just a few days, I began to have second, third, fourth, and yes, fifth thoughts about my impromptu decision.

I could already see the headline of the local newspaper: "Former Nurse Executive Trades Hospital Position for Door-to-Door Sales Job." Or better still, "Local Female Pastor, Grandmother, Well Known Community Leader, and Winner of Many Honors and Awards Admitted to Psychiatric Hospital for Bizarre Behavior." I felt certain my children would gladly corroborate any negative information printed in the paper and also assist as I was placed in a straitjacket to be taken to the local psychiatry hospital. Most of all, I feared what my congregation, Alpha Kappa Alpha Sorority members, Leadership Memphis classmates, and my four newly acquired sons-in-law would think when they heard I had lost my mind. However, I never doubted that my husband would stand by me (even though he might also think I was crazy).

To confirm my own suspicion about my sanity and arouse more of others' curiosity I—without prior warning or discussion—called a local auction company, packed up all of the clothing in my dress shop, and sent my inventory to be auctioned to the highest bidder. It was not easy, but I closed the doors to what had been a growing and very successful small business. All of this was done in a matter of five days.

My family, friends, and customers were in shock when they discovered what I had done. I must admit, I was too! There were two questions everyone asked me: "Why did you do it?" and "Why so quickly?" My answer was, "God told me to do it." No one dared to argue with that answer.

Not only had I closed my successful business of eighteen years (with nine years being in the same location), but over night I was rapidly losing weight from using my products. The sudden closing of my business and the almost overnight, drastic weight loss were two occurrences that made my decision to go full time into network marketing all the more questionable.

Was I sane or insane? I asked myself this as more friends called to inquire, "What are you doing?" "Why have you closed your business?" "Why are you losing so much weight?" The questions were endless, and I was vacillating between excitement and doubt.

However, to my surprise, several friends of long standing who believed I was not crazy saw my rapid weight loss, bought the products, and immediately joined the business. They stated that their reason for coming into the company to work with me was simple: they believed in me and did not think that I would sell them anything that would hurt them. I was humbled by my friends' confidence, especially since I had joined the company without having tasted the products. I was also humbled because three or four of these new recruits had followed me into three other unsuccessful network marketing ventures, so I was amazed that they still felt that I had integrity and was a creditable leader. I was energized by their faith in me and encouraged to see if I could really build a team at my age. However, some doubt remained.

The minor success of signing up four people at the top level within one month was enough to light the fire under me, earn for me a handsome $1,600 bonus, and start me thinking, "I can do this business!" The promise of four additional people to sign up before the end of the next month was incredible and served as confirmation that God had truly led me into the network marketing business. Yep, God was in this for sure!

Certainly, my role model, Moses, must have experienced similar feelings of inadequacy when he was sent by God to tell Pharaoh to let the children of Israel leave Egypt to journey to the land of Canaan. I can imagine how stupid he must have felt standing before Pharaoh saying, "God told me to tell you to let His people go." However, God provided the miracles Moses needed in order to achieve his mission. Moses and the people were set free, and he was allowed to lead them from Egypt toward the Promised Land. At no time did Moses rely upon himself to perform that difficult task. God brought about the miracles that resulted in their release and their ultimate pilgrimage.

But I had to face the fact that I was in the middle of my challenge and not in the process of being led out of it, and I was not aware of a miracle being planned for me. The realization that I really did not know what I was doing was finally sinking in; the resulting "fake-it-until-you-make-it" act could only work for so long. The constant vacillating between "Do I really want to do this?" and "I can do this?" had to be resolved very quickly since, for some reason, my team was rapidly growing.

The passion I had for the products and the results I and others had experienced were phenomenal. When I stepped on my bathroom scales and saw that I had lost 17 pounds and 2 dress sizes in 10 days I knew that I could and would work the business! My mind was made up, and my motives for doing the business changed. I reasoned, if the products had been highly effective for me, then they would also be effective for and a blessing to others.

Not only did my husband and I lose tremendous weight, but both of us quickly experienced very positive physical changes and an immediate decrease in the health problems we had been plagued with for years. I knew many potential clients with the same or similar health problems as our own. As a result, I vowed to help them as much as I could.

The decision to build a team became a necessity. I no longer sought to "work the business" as a means to gain personal financial freedom. Instead, I knew that the best way to help combat obesity and decrease many of the related health challenges was to educate people and get as many of them as possible involved in my new business. Very quickly my motivation and purpose changed from personally losing weight and making a lot of money to helping others to gain financial freedom and lose weight. No one told me that in doing so I would also remarkably improve my own finances.

As my passion for the products and the company grew, so did my team and my finances. Soon, I was faced with a major problem: I could not continue all of my pursuits. My team was growing, and I was the leader. As the leader, I knew that I needed to learn the business.

By now my team and I were selling weight loss products very well. However, we did not know about all of the other wonderful health enhancing products the company offered; We knew so little about the company—not the names of its founder and president nor even where it was located—because I had not read the manual. I was busy recruiting people, and

17

we were selling products like crazy. Sure, I knew how to sell the product but I didn't know a thing about the company's policies and procedures. What was in the blue book that I received in the box with my original product orders? When would I start weekly training classes for my team? How would I train people I had recruited into the business that lived in other cities? I was being asked so many hard questions. I began to ask myself questions, such as, "Are all new recruits in my city, my responsibility?" I thought they were. "Will they stay with the team or leave?" "What am I going to do?"

By this time people were calling me their "upline!"[1] I knew I needed to get more information on the company and the products in order to be able to help others and myself. But how would I get this valuable information? Who would I turn to? What would I do? These were just a few more of the questions I asked myself. Somewhere, I read that success is a process, not an overnight payoff. You must work at becoming all you can become. The person that sponsored me, Gailey Ward, was a new distributor, herself; therefore, she was unable to help me with the multitude of questions that flooded my mind and left me very confused. However, she did provide me with the names and telephone numbers of two prominent people in her upline. I called both of them.

Finally, after several attempts, I connected with two upline couples in the company who knew more than I did. Both couples were successfully working the business and were

---

[1] For those who are unfamiliar with the term, an "upline" in network marketing is a distributor's sponsor; a "downline" is a person who has signed up to be a distributor working under someone who already is a distributor.

very highly respected. I was on my way! All I needed was for someone to point me to the top! When I called the two couples for assistance—Eileen Silva and her husband Taylor Heagan, Crown Presidential Directors, and Billy Banks and his wife Eltha Banks, Presidential Directors—they immediately took me under their wings. Eileen consented to serve as my mentor to help me master the art of becoming successful in the company.

It was hard, but I was learning through past episodes and failures that I needed to be coachable if I wanted to become a successful leader. When I was in a prior company I felt it was necessary and important for my team to "do things my way." To my dismay, before long my small downline was not interested in being bossed by me, and only one person was working. I guess I just could not seem to make the transition from nursing management to encouraging each person to become his or her own boss.

That short lived venture left me in more than $20,000 debt because I had also made the mistake of trying to purchase enough products each month to maintain the volumes required to retain my management level position. I had achieved two levels in management within my first three months in the company. Soon I found myself in a dilemma and desperate to maintain my dwindling Area Manager income.

Afraid of failure, as well as not wanting to let down my dear friend, Shelley (Phillipy) Baur, who was my immediate upline, I continuously bought products in large quantities. As a result, I charged products on three of my credit cards and quickly reached the maximum limits. I was in such desperation that I repeatedly had the limits raised on each card in further attempts to retain my level and help my friend Shelley, who was at that time a Vice President. I rationalized by telling myself that I was only doing this until I could recruit more people for my team. Not until it was too late did I understand what I had done was a definite no-no, and it was a sure way to go bankrupt or very deeply into debt.

I thought I would be able to save face and eventually earn a lot of quick money, but instead, my team crumpled. My once loyal and supportive distributors left the business when they discovered that network marketing was not the fastest way in the world to make money. I truly bought a very expensive lesson in how not to do network marketing.

Before long it became quite obvious to me that the failure was my fault. The company leaders and my upline were wonderful, the products were great, but try as I may, I just could not seem to retain a customer base nor build a good downline. I attended every training that I could, made lifelong friends, won several small prizes and certificates, and was even an on-stage winner at the national convention. Yet, hard as I tried, I failed at becoming a successful network marketer.

Finally, I dropped downward a level, and my monthly check went from an all- time high of $900 per month to $100 or less. It was at that point that I decided to give the business up but continue using the products (because they were excellent products). At that point, I surmised that I should also give up trying to build a team.

With my decision made, I turned my attention back to more familiar, tried and true ways of making a living. I never fully understood why I had failed because I thought I had done everything it took to be successful. I had the desire, passion, product knowledge, respect for my upline, and determination needed to work the business, but for some reason, I had not been successful nor prosperous. I reprimanded myself by saying, "I must have lost my mind because fifty-eight years old is usually not the age most people would be going into network marketing for the first time." I felt like getting my head examined.

Three years later, I was sixty-one years old and ready to try it again. I said to myself, "I must be a glutton for punishment, or I have really and truly lost my mind," especially since I had no cash on hand. I had to use a portion of my retirement and meager savings in order to acquire the total startup money I needed to enter First Fitness International at the top entry level. I decided that if I was going to do the business Gailey introduced to me, I might as well do it right and start at the top. Because of my last three disastrous ventures, I did not tell my husband what start up had cost me, nor where I had gotten the money for the business. I did not want him to think that this new business would also fail.

What a good feeling it was when less than two weeks into the business I not only had repeat business, but I was receiving customers by referral. This was too good to be true. Friends joined me in the business, and they recruited other distributors as well. I finally had my network marketing team going. This time, I vowed, I would do it right.

One of the reasons for my being unsuccessful in the prior network marketing attempt was that I refused to be coachable and allow Shelley to help me. I thought that I already knew what to do and how to do it. It finally sank in that being coachable was really the primary ingredient for making bricks (especially when you know nothing about how to make them).

Being self-motivated, adventurous (despite my age), and passionate about the products, I registered to attend one of the organization's training sessions in Detroit, Michigan. It was exactly three weeks after I had joined First Fitness International as a Super Star at the Director level. Now, for the first time, I would learn how to build and train a team.

In Detroit, I met Lee Causey, Founder, and Nigel Branson, President of First Fitness International. I was mesmerized by their leadership abilities and friendliness. The two men were very articulate and dedicated to the success of both their distributors and their company. The training was one of the best I had ever attended. It was there in Detroit, that I heard incredible product success testimonies and also witnessed one couple achieve Crown Presidential Director, the highest level in the company.

Even though I had gone to Detroit alone and knew no one in the company except my immediate upline (whom I had seen only one time), I did not feel alone. The classes and information were easy to comprehend, and the fellowship with other distributors was great. I returned to Memphis uplifted. I internalized every bit of information given to me and was completely motivated to go to the top. In addition, I collected the business cards of every person who said, "If you need my help, call me."

Yet, instead of eagerly rushing to make my fortune, I sat down and developed a training guide and regular meeting schedule for my team. I wrote my mission statement and purpose for doing the business, along with the names of fifty people that I thought might be interested in working with me. The list of names was developed from names of former neighbors, organizations, high school classmates, family reunion members, my old telephone books, and local newspapers.

After compiling the list, I purchased six books by some of the leading network marketing authors and four tapes from outstanding motivational speakers. I was determined to better understand how to build a strong team and have a viable, home based, network marketing business. Things began to fall into place, and I began to build a *real team*. I realized that I did want to become successful in network marketing. I decided to go for it!

Now, two years later, with much effort, I have finally

overcome my previous failures, and I am doing the work that it takes to become successful. This time, I have no problems with being coachable. As a matter of fact, I frequently telephone my uplines Eileen and Taylor, and Billy and Eltha, for assistance. Participating in national conference calls and making my presence known in the company by winning trips and awards for achieving high volumes and increased recruitment have helped me to be viewed as a leader in First Fitness. But nothing has compared with the experience that I gained from doing the business all wrong.

However, had I initially looked at network marketing as a profession and a business, worked it like a business, and been coachable, maybe (just maybe) I would not have had to start over at age sixty-one. On the other hand, if I had not failed in my previous attempts I may never have found the wonderful products and business opportunity that First Fitness offered. Just think of what I would have missed.

"All things [do] work together for the good of those who love the Lord and are the called according to His purpose."
Romans 8:28

Are You Crazy?

"An Invitation"

Send Me, I'll Go.

Chapter 3

The Making of a Miracle

(Nehemiah, the Great Miracle Worker)

Even though Moses was the first biblical person to work miracles and was the person of God to capture my attention as a role model, Nehemiah was another effective biblical leader who was very successful in demonstrating how God works to accomplish the impossible.

I am convinced that compassion, commitment, passionate desire, and dedication are the foundations and essential ingredients that must be present in great quantities when straw is not available for building bricks. Nehemiah was faced with such a task. And, like when Moses needed help, God intervened and prevailed by performing a miracle in order to assure Nehemiah's success.

Nehemiah was deeply touched, but he was motivated into action when he heard that his kindred remained in captivity in "great affliction and reproach" (Nehemiah 1:3). I will not try to tell the entire story, but Nehemiah sat down and wept, mourned, and fasted for days, praying to God about the devastation and the destruction of his people and the city of Jerusalem.

Nehemiah asked God to grant him favor that the king might give him permission to leave the palace and his position as the king's cup bearer to go back to rebuild Jerusalem, the city where his fathers were buried (Nehemiah 2). The first hint of the making of a miracle was that the king actually granted Nehemiah's request. It was highly unlikely that a king would allow his personal cup bearer to leave his side for such an unusual journey, especially since the cup bearer was the most trusted servant in the king's palace. This trusted servant was the person who tasted food and drink prior to the king's partaking of them in order to assure that they were not harmful. However, Nehemiah wanted to go, so he prayed for favor and for God to prosper him, and God granted his request. Reading chapters five and six of Nehemiah helped me to understand the dynamics of moving the mighty hand of God in order to receive and accomplish a miracle.

Nehemiah is also very effective in demonstrating how to accomplish the impossible through soliciting and properly utilizing the strengths and skills of others. I have not seen nor have I heard of examples of teamwork greater than those displayed in the fourth and fifth chapters of the book of Nehemiah: "for the people had a mind to work" (4:6), and they worked together. This book of the Bible provides an excellent lesson in networking and teaches us how to get work done with the assistance of others.

Nehemiah is also an excellent example of how the leader must articulate his or her mission and vision urgently, clearly, and very passionately in order to get followers to accept ownership and to work as one to achieve the desired goal. Nehemiah possessed all of the essential qualities of leadership that I have detailed. As a result of prayer, he moved both God and man to help him in his quest to build the wall that had been destroyed.

The Bible says in Nehemiah 2:1-3, that Nehemiah was clearly and deeply saddened when he heard that his kindred remained in captivity and in great affliction. The wall of Jerusalem was broken down, and the gates to the entrance of that great and marvelous city had been burned with fire. The news must have been very hurting and depressing to this great man who loved God, his people, and the place where he was born. In Nehemiah 1:4, the Bible says, Nehemiah sat down and wept, mourned, fasted, and prayed before the God of Heaven. He prayed about the sin, devastation, and destruction of the people and the city. Then, Nehemiah prayed and asked God to grant him favor with the king. Not only did the king send Nehemiah back to Jerusalem but he also sent letters to be given to the governors requesting materials for the work that had to be done. It is written that Nehemiah said, *". . . And the King granted me according to the good hand of my God upon me"* (2:8). As if that were not enough, the Bible says: *". . . Now the king had sent captains of the army and horsemen with me"* (2:9).

Without a doubt God was on his side, and Nehemiah

was being divinely sent on a mission for the purpose of accomplishing God's ultimate plan for his life. Nehemiah probably thought that he would serve in the king's palace as cup bearer for his entire life, but God had a greater work for him. God needed Nehemiah for leadership and for restoring the wall around Jerusalem. The mission appeared to be impossible. Nehemiah's situation required a miracle. Who would help him? How long would he be absent from the king's palace? How would he find the materials he needed? Each question required an answer that Nehemiah could not provide. The entire situation was a "God thing." If God did not provide the people, the materials, and touch the king's heart to grant him a sabbatical, Nehemiah could not be successful.

Sometimes I believe we are allowed to experience a similar situation so God can demonstrate "His power" to provide. God gave Nehemiah the mission, purpose, and vision; however, the leadership ability and favor with others was just as important to his success. In Nehemiah 2:18, we see God's favor and His gift of leadership ability being put into action by Nehemiah.

There were people in Nehemiah's day as there are today who, shortly after others make a commitment to do a task, predict that their undertaking will fail. Sometimes, friends (and even loved ones) will laugh at our efforts. Nevertheless, the purpose and mission must be foremost; we must stay focused knowing that God has ordained and will prosper the work.

Nehemiah and the builders of the wall were just a part of a miracle designed and implemented by God. It all started with the prayer that Nehemiah prayed in chapter 1 verses 6 and 11: *"Let thine ear now be attentive, and thine eyes open, that thou mayest hear the prayer of thy servant, which I pray before thee now, day and night, for the children of Israel thy servants, and confess the sins of the children of Israel, which we have sinned against thee: both I and my father's house have sinned. . . . O Lord, I beseech thee, let now thine ear be attentive to the prayer of thy servant, and to the prayer of thy servants, who desire to fear thy name: and prosper, I pray thee, thy servant this day, and grant him many in the sight of this man [the king]. . . ."*

God is still a prayer answering God, and He knows what we have need of before we ever ask. Could it be that you have not succeeded in your work or business because you failed to ask for divine intervention? Prayer is the beginning of the miracle.

"The Lord is far from the wicked: but he heareth the prayer of the righteous."
Proverbs 15:29

Find Your Wall

Chapter 4

Finding Your Wall

(Where is Your Area of Leadership?)

When you feel God has called you to share in the ministry of outreach to His people, there should be no excuses for not answering His call. Of course, you have to choose whether or not you will go into the vineyard as a leader to start your own work, or whether you will help build a work that someone else has initiated. Whatever the choice, the responsibility for getting started, staying on purpose, and completing the mission cannot be given to anyone else. When God calls you to do a work, the work is yours to perform. But with God's blessings, you can allow others to share in the work within the perimeters that God allows.

Ministries are areas of Christian service to humankind that exemplify and edify the kingdom here on earth; these ministries provide opportunities for God to work through those who are willing to be used by Him. Most people wait for the call before they seek to find the area of ministry that best allows them to utilize their gifts and talents. It does not matter whether the ministry is within or outside the church. However, there is usually no blueprint for success given to those whom

God calls and sends. The only thing we can be assured of is, God will go with us to instruct and guide us (if we allow Him). In the interim, we must pray for God's direction and follow His instructions in order to become successful in fulfilling our assignments.

The most difficult part of entering the ministry is accurately determining one's area of service or not wanting to work in the area of God's choosing. We really wish He would change His mind, send us in another area, or just leave us alone to do whatever it is that we are comfortable doing. When the area of service becomes clear to you—no matter how long it takes—God alleviates your fears, He gets you settled, and He readies you to do the task. The way to accomplish the assignment appears to flow with little or no difficulty.

When Moses stopped protesting about his assignment and accepted Aaron as his support person, he was able to go unto Pharaoh with a powerful message from God. When Joshua received and accepted the assurance that as God was with Moses, so would He be with him, Joshua was able to take over the leadership after the death of Moses and complete Moses' assignment. When Jeremiah realized that God did not care that he was just a young boy and that he was indeed being called and sent as a prophet, he began to function in that role. If Jeremiah had asked others for their opinions rather than doing what God had instructed him to do, I feel certain their responses would have discouraged and/or stopped him because certainly the others would have told Jeremiah that he was too young.

Almost daily I am asked, "How do you do so many things at one time?" and "How do you do so many things well?" My answer to the questions is, "I never ask permission or need validation from others to do what God has told me to do. I just do it."

I begin all of my assignments prayerfully and quickly, keeping my mission and purpose foremost in my mind. When God speaks, I move! Prayer and swiftness are my two reasons for being successfully multi-tasked. Sometimes, to others it may appear as if I'm doing in excess of three or four things at a time, but I really am not. I use my time effectively and efficiently. I stay on purpose in order to be able to get more accomplished. The ability to stay focused is one of my greatest assets. In order to accomplish great things you must learn to stay on purpose and remain focused on the task at hand until it is completed.

However, I cannot minimize the fact that finding where you are supposed to be and being sure beyond a shadow of a doubt that you are in divine order is usually not easily accomplished. The work must wait until your mission and purpose are clear. Passion and perseverance will develop within you when your desire is to be obedient and pleasing to God. When you wait for directions your mission and purpose will be in alignment with His will and plan for your life.

Nehemiah's work was to rebuild the wall around Jerusalem. In 1999, God gave me "a wall to rebuild" as well. My wall was to build confidence and trust within people in order to introduce them to the life changing benefits of my health and wellness products.

The challenge included being able to support and inspire my clients to remain on the products and eating plan until they reached their weight goal. The more overweight the client had become or the more attempts the client had made and failed, the greater was my challenge.

Long before I ever heard of First Fitness International, God equipped me for my ministry through my background in leadership, pastoral care, nursing, education, and counseling, coupled with my experience of dramatic success with the product. The product had significantly decreased my blood pressure, eliminated the arthritic pain in my knees and hands, and eliminated my sinus and allergic reactions. The significant changes in my health made me a noticeable witness to the product's effectiveness and enabled me to help others to help themselves and to make the lifestyle changes needed to improve their quality of life.

I have come full circle by gaining extensive knowledge and experience in several professions. These varied experiences have ultimately resulted in my being able to tear down walls of distrust and rebuild lasting relationships with my clients. As a result of building excellent trust relationships with my clients I have been able to help hundreds of people achieve their dreams and regain their lives. Likewise, I attribute my ability and success in building a strong team to values, goals, and the gift of leadership that God gave me. I give God all the glory, for without Him I would be nothing.

A wall awaits each of you. God has work for you to do. The Bible says: *"Ask, and it shall be given you; seek, and ye shall find; knock, and it shall be opened unto you: for everyone that asketh receiveth; and he that seeketh findeth; and to him that knocketh it shall be opened"* (Matthew 7:7-8). You have but to ask! God is ready to reveal His purpose, plan, and "wall" to you if you are ready to work.

Thou therefore gird up thy loins, and arise, and speak unto them all that I command thee: be not dismayed at their faces, lest I confound thee before them. For behold, I have made thee this day a defenced city, and an iron pillar, and brazen walls against the whole land, against the kings of Judah, against the princes thereof, against the priests thereof, and against the people of the land. And they shall fight against thee; but they shall not prevail against thee; for I am with thee, saith the Lord, to deliver thee (Jeremiah 1:17-19).

Your ministry may not be in health and wellness. However, God has the perfect ministry for you. Do not spend time worrying about finding it. Jesus gives the answer in Matthew 6:27-34; your assurance is in the last two verses (verses 33 and 34): *"But seek ye first the kingdom of God, and His righteousness; and all these things shall be added unto you. Take therefore no thought for the morrow: for the morrow shall take thought for the things of itself. Sufficient unto the day is the evil thereof."* If you really do want to know what your ministry is and will present your body unto

37

the Lord for His use, the Lord will reveal His plan to you.

Neither Nehemiah, Moses, Joshua, nor any of the other great leaders and prophets in the Bible went looking to try to find something to do for God. When our desire is to serve, God knows where we should serve and how our gifts and talents can best be utilized. Ask Him! Wherever God places you will be the ideal area of service for you. And you will feel good about it, do extremely well, help others, be personally satisfied, and most of all, God will get the glory from your efforts. When each of these things occurs you will have received confirmation that you have found your "wall" in ministry. Working on it will lead you to a feeling of self-actualization and success.

Remember; no one and nothing can stop you or your progress but you. Become a modern-day Nehemiah; find your area of ministry; then, rediscover and use your gifts and talents in your work. There is ministry that needs to be done all around you. It is not hard to see or to do when you truly become a servant of God and a servant to others. Little does become much when you place your work and yourself in the Master's hand. If you are a builder you should be building. If you are a leader then you should be leading. If you are seeking God for your wall in order to become a servant leader, please know for a certainty that God is seeking you. Just be patient and have a mind to work. God will reveal His plan for you and give you a wall to work on that will cause others to marvel in astonishment at your ability and your ultimate success.

"What shall we then say to these things?
If God be for us, who can be against us?"
Romans 8:31

Why ME?

WHY ME? I ASKED. WHY NOT? HE SAID.
I can use even you.
Everyone can help to get the job done
there's so much yet to do.
WHY ME? I ASKED. WHY NOT? HE SAID.
I gave you talents many.
Just put them all to use for me
And work until the finish.
WHY ME? I ASKED. WHY NOT? HE SAID.
You promised you would serve.
Now preach and pray to help the lost
And keep my every word.
WHY ME? I ASKED. WHY NOT? HE SAID.
There are sick ones to be healed.
Loneliness, sorrow, sadness, and sin
Have sapped my children's will.
WHY ME? I ASKED. WHY NOT? HE SAID.
You're the best I have today.
The people need a guiding light
To help them find their way.
WHY ME? I ASKED. WHY NOT? HE SAID.
Go see what you can do.
Don't worry, come what may my child
For I am sending you!

Brick By Brick

Chapter 5

Build the Wall Brick by Brick

(Building in Spite of Opposition and Obstacles)

Even though Nehemiah's mission and purpose was to make beautiful again the wall of Jerusalem and help the people, everyone was not happy and supportive of him. When Sanballat, Tobiah, and Geshem heard of his plan they were exceedingly angry. These men did not want Nehemiah to be successful. They made fun of Nehemiah and tried to stop the rebuilding of the wall.

Nehemiah took a few men with him and was careful not to tell anyone what God had inspired him to do at Jerusalem. Nehemiah's mission and purpose was divinely inspired. Going out by the cover of night, he surveyed the damage and made a mental picture of what was to be accomplished. He conceived a plan. The plan was essential in order to rebuild the broken down walls and to replace the gates, which had been burned by fire. Afterwards, Nehemiah returned to the parent group. No one knew where he had been, not even the priests, nobles, and rulers, nor the people that were to assist him in the rebuilding. Nehemiah did not know about the modern term "dream stealers," but he knew as a leader, he could not share his vision, mission, purpose or plan with the entire group because everyone was not spiritually mature enough nor mentally and physically prepared to undertake so great a challenge. Nehemiah already had a well defined plan.

As I read the first and second chapters of Nehemiah I reflected on the responses of some of my friends and family when I began my First Fitness business. I should have re-read Nehemiah prior to announcing my new venture. I am sure I could have prepared myself for much of the negative and unsolicited input that I received.

Eventually, Nehemiah did approach the entire group with his plans. He called them to action in a concerted effort to get the mission accomplished. His detailed description of the challenge was magnified when he told the people: *". . . Ye see the distress that we are in, how Jerusalem lieth waste, and the gates thereof are burned with fire: come and let us build up the wall of Jerusalem that we be no more a reproach"* (Nehemiah 2:17). Then Nehemiah told them of the hand of God which was upon him and how the king had granted him permission to accomplish the task of rebuilding the wall of Jerusalem. Nehemiah made it clear that he would not attempt the feat without their help.

The people's response to Nehemiah was *"let us rise up and build"* (2:18), so they strengthened their hands for the work. For they perceived Nehemiah to be their leader and believed the work had been ordained of God. Most people will work if their leader has integrity and the reward for completing the mission is gratifying and satisfying.

Just knowing that God sent Nehemiah to perform the work would have been motivating enough to get me involved. Being able to see the walls and gates almost repaired and standing as a testimony of what had been accomplished would have been the only powerful, sustaining evidence I would have needed in order to stay focused until the task reached completion. Evidently, Nehemiah and the workers were able to work together toward a common goal. The "what," "when," and "how" never superseded their "why." As a result, Nehemiah and the workers were able to start and finish a task that others may have considered impossible.

Most projects undertaken with determination, however, attract either a Sanballat, Tobiah, and Geshem, or a group of people waiting to laugh at and scorn the hard worker into quitting. Nehemiah did not listen to the heckling, nor did he waste time responding to their stupid questions. His response to their question, *"What is this thing that you do?"* was, *". . . The God of Heaven, he will prosper us; therefore we his servants will arise and build . . . "* (2:20). In other words, he was saying, "God sent us, and told us what to do, and we are going to do what God has given us to do!" Nehemiah knew his purpose and was clear about his mission.

The third chapter of Nehemiah expounds upon the second miracle that I saw while reading: teamwork that is matchless. I could clearly see God at work in each phase of the building process.

43

"Then Eliashib the high priest rose up with his brethren the priests, and they builded the sheep gate; they sanctified it, and set up the doors of it; . . . And next unto him builded the men of Jericho. And next to them builded Zaccur the son of Imri. But the fish gate did the sons of Hassenaah build, who also laid the beams thereof, and set up the doors thereof, the locks thereof, and the bars thereof. And next unto them repaired . . . Zadok the son of Baana. And next unto them the Tekoites repaired; but their nobles put not their necks to the work of their lord. Moreover the old gate repaired Jehoiada the son of Paseah, and Meshullam the son of Besodeiah; they laid the beams thereof, and set up the doors thereof, and the locks thereof, and the bars thereof. . . ."

"After him repaired Meshullam the son of Berechia over against his chamber. After him repaired Malchiah the goldsmith's son unto the place of the Nethinims, and of the merchants, over against the gate Miphkad, and to the going up of the corner. And between the going up of the corner unto the sheep gate repaired the goldsmiths and the merchants" (from Nehemiah, Chapter 3).

It is important to notice in reading through Chapter 3 that "everybody" worked! The educated, the wealthy, the priest, and others of status worked alongside their family members and those of higher or lower estate. The assignments were given to them according to the work that needed to be done and their level of expertise, not by hierarchy. Nehemiah utilized every available person in order to complete the building of the wall within the time constraints he had established with the king.

I do believe, and have often heard it said, "People will work harder for praises than for raises." The people that assisted nehemiah in rebuilding the wall did not do it for pay. Instead, they did it for "their city." They did it for the satisfaction of seeing the restoration complete and the personal joy and pride that was derived from knowing that they had done their jobs well.

I am of the opinion that personal achievement and satisfaction is more of a driver than money for many people. On stage recognition, five-star trips, gifts, and elaborate publicity have motivated more people than can be imagined to excel and achieve top positions in network marketing. Whatever the incentive, whether it is provided on the job, at church, by a social club, or other entity, most people want to achieve it.

Nehemiah 6:15-16 says, *"So the wall was finished in the twenty and fifth day of the month Elul, in fifty and two days. And it came to pass, that when all our enemies heard thereof, and all the heathen that were about us saw these things, they were much cast down in their own eyes: for they perceived that this work was wrought of our God."*

Building by Faith

Nehemiah's men worked upon the wall
While Sanballat mocked to say
"These feeble Jews can't finish!
It will never last a day.

If a fox ran up he'd beak it
Even though it's made of stone
Work as hard as you will or may
It will never last for long."

Nevertheless: they prayed to God
Throughout their awful plight
As the enemy tried to hinder them
They worked both day and night.

Half of the servants were able to work
While half held spears and bows
Under the watchful eyes of God they labored
They worked despite their foes.

Nehemiah said "Our God will fight
For us the work is great
Take not off your clothes by day
Except to wash, don't wait."

So they labored on the burned down wall
To prove Sanballat had lied
The enemy thought it could not be done
But God was on their side.

They rebuilt the wall by faith
And left no breach within
And after the work was finished
It stood where rubbish had been.

Back At The Red Sea

Chapter 6

Back at the Red Sea

Moses went back down into Egypt to deliver the Israelites. Even though a part of the land of Egypt was called Memphis, it definitely was not Memphis, Tennessee. Moses' task was to lead the children of Israel out of bondage, away from the cruelty of Pharaoh and on into Caanan, which was the "Promised Land". God called Moses and anointed him to his task of leadership at a time when a strong, bold, courageous leader was badly needed. However, the people grumbled and rebelled as Moses attempted to keep them focused and lead them to a land they were either not able to visualize or were too fearful to enter.

It did not matter that Moses tried to prove that the mighty hand of God was over them and guiding them; fear and dread constantly fell upon the Israelites, and they preferred to turn back and go into Egypt, from which God had just delivered them, rather than to go forward to safety and freedom. Exodus 16:1-3, relates how the whole congregation of the children of Israel murmured against Moses and Aaron in the wilderness, and the children of Israel said to them: *". . . Would to God we had died by the hand of the Lord in the land of Egypt, when we sat by the flesh pots, and when we did eat bread to the full; for ye have brought us forth into this wilderness, to kill this whole assembly with hunger"* (v.3). As in prior times, though angered by their constant murmurings, God provided. *"And Moses said, This shall be, when the Lord shall give you in the evening flesh to eat, and in the morning bread to the full; for that the Lord heareth your murmurings which ye murmur against him: and what are we? Your murmurings are not against us, but against the Lord"* (Exodus 16:8).

Surely Moses was saddened by their constant murmuring, especially since he had done his best to get the people to look back and remember the mercy and goodness of God. Exodus 14:10-14, states,

> *"And when Pharaoh drew nigh, the children of Israel lifted up their eyes, and, behold, the Egyptians marched after them; and they were sore afraid: and the children of Israel cried out unto the Lord. And they said unto Moses, Because there were no graves in Egypt, hast thou taken us away to die in the wilderness? Wherefore hast thou dealt thus with us, to carry us forth out of Egypt? Is not this the word we did tell thee in Egypt, saying, Let us alone, that we may serve the Egyptians? For it had been better for us to serve the Egyptians, than that we should die in the wilderness. And Moses said unto the people, Fear ye not, stand still, and see the*

salvation of the Lord, which he will show to you today: for the Egyptians whom ye have seen today, ye shall see them again no more for ever. The Lord shall fight for you, and ye shall hold your peace."

God did indeed fight for them, and their enemies were drowned in the Red Sea.

God saved the Israelites, but Moses had the hard task of keeping them moving and going forward toward the sea instead of backward toward Egypt. The Israelites murmured and complained every step of the way as they went toward the miracle God had already prepared for them. Reaching the "Promised Land" was intended to take only an eleven-day journey across the wilderness; instead, it took forty years to get there.

There is no doubt in my mind that God changed the direction of my ministry and my life. In doing so, I inherited a similar peril of leadership as Moses experienced. It did not take me long to realize that people are often excited and happy when they begin a new experience; usually they are optimistic and positive. My challenge, like Moses's, came when new distributors did not build a team or sell their product as quickly as they had planned. Their vision of getting rich quick soon disintegrated, and then negative self-talk and murmuring began. More distributors than I would like to remember said, "I need to send my pack back. I can't sell this stuff." Their personal weight loss success was not enough to motivate them to continue working their business. Seeing other distributors and me successfully working the business did not increase their desire to work more effectively and efficiently. Attending new distributor classes and weekly opportunity meetings also failed to inspire them to become productive or to gain a positive attitude. These modern-day Israelites were acting very akin to the group Moses was challenged to lead.

Clearly, several of the murmurers were in immediate need of a financial blessing. It was obvious to me by their conversations that what they had been doing to earn a living was not yielding enough income to meet their monthly obligations. However, they were not committed enough to "trust the process" and stick with the company until their team could begin to grow and their income increase. Getting frustrated and fearful only caused them to have poorer performance, and before long it was as if I was between Egypt and the Red Sea, and like Moses, I needed God to work a miracle or my team would rapidly be dissolved. Shortly thereafter, weekly meetings were only attended by a few faithful distributors who had been with me in a prior company. Every encouraging thing I tried to say seemed to fall on deaf ears. No amount of prodding or begging or assisting them gave me the results I desired. Finally, as a result of the complaining and negativism, I had to reassess my strategies, my team, and my abilities. Desirous of becoming a Presidential Director in the First Fitness leadership team, I had to come up with a solution quickly, or I would never reach my goal within the time I had allotted.

I prayed. Like Moses, I could see God at work for these distributors, but they could not. I knew that if they worked as if the business was their primary source of income, it would eventually pay them like a business. But as much as I wanted them to become successful these murmurers steadfastly complained, "I'm not making enough money," "Too many people are saying no," and "I don't know who to sell the products to or where to find recruits." I was at my wit's end. Even though I had been recruiting new distributors and selling large amounts of products, I felt as if I was a failure as well. The stress of trying to turn negative people into positive people began to drain my energy. Soon, it was a chore just trying to keep myself motivated. Yet, I knew God was faithful. Therefore, I continued to pray daily and ask God for wisdom in order to build a strong team. I knew from my previous ventures that I must build a strong, supportive, productive, team in order to go upward in the organization, and to maintain my position. The few, faithful distributors I had on the team (that were working) were not building widely nor deeply enough to help take me to the next level. At times it appeared to me that I was the only one working. However, I knew that I was not alone. What I needed, I thought, was a good old fashioned Red Sea miracle! I didn't care how God chose to do it; He could part the Red Sea for me, take me around it, or over it. It did not matter; I just wanted Him to do something, and do it real quick!

As I sat at my desk one day pondering the situation, my eyes fell upon the book, *My First Year in MLM*, by Mark and Renee' Yarnell. I picked it up and began to thumb through it, half reading its content, when I came across the startling words that approximately 60 percent of all new recruits would leave the business within the first year. I re-read, the sentence wondering if the writer had actually written what I thought I had read. Then I remembered my trip to Detroit, Michigan, that I had taken shortly after joining the company. It was there that I heard Crown Presidential Directors Moses and Dolleen Wilson say the one thing that they would do differently was to "not keep calling, prodding, and trying to get people to work the business." Dolleen spoke clearly that it was "better to get new people than to keep on trying to get people to do the business that do not want to do it." I had the answer! I needed to do what God told Moses to do in Exodus 14:15: *"And the Lord said unto Moses, Wherefore criest thou unto me? Speak unto the children of Israel, that they go forward."* I needed to go forward!

Within three months of almost losing my team, I was successful in becoming a Presidential Director. The position was indeed earned within the time I had allotted. God did not part the Red Sea for me, but God did revive within me the motivation needed to do what I could do to move myself to the next level. I chose to go out and recruit new energetic, excited people and ignore the grumbling, murmuring, and complaining of those who were unhappy and unproductive. In record breaking time I was on an upward climb helping those who still wanted to work and those who were new and adventurous enough to try. Needless to say, the positive energy of my new people and the success I was experiencing in my own First Fitness business resulted in some of the less productive people becoming more committed, and much of the murmuring ceased. When I trusted enough to be willing to "let go and let God," I no longer needed a miracle; I just needed to recruit people to my team that wanted to go with me to the "Promised Land."

God has already promised to do more for us than we can think or ask. He just seems to respond much quicker when we need Him and ask. The only reason I felt that I was back at the Red Sea and in need of a miracle was that I started focusing on the situation rather than focusing on the solution.

The Answer To The Secret

Chapter 7

The Stress, the Struggle, and the Secret

The stress of being self-employed or of being an active network marketer is usually self induced. It is frequently due to unnecessary worrying about not progressing as rapidly as the new entrepreneur anticipated and/or living with a poverty mentality. "Stinking Thinking" proclaims only failure, gloom, and doom, "I will not have enough income," and/or a million other frightening "what if's." Nine times out of ten, the "what if's" will never happen, and income will eventually increase if more attention is directed toward working the business rather than worrying about the business.

The less the new distributor worries about the profit and the more he or she concentrates on the "why" for working the business, the more the business will yield on-purpose and mission driven results. Planned, purposeful, and meaningful activities are necessary in order to decrease many of the stressors that divert focus and activity from work to self and financial needs.

Stress is a killer. Stress is also an enemy and stealer of time and joy. God never intended that we should carry our own burdens and shoulder our own cares. In I Peter 5:7, the Bible reminds us that God wants us to give every care and concern to Him: *". . . Casting all your care upon Him for he careth for you."* I heard someone say, "When network marketing ceases to be fun, the person is doing it all wrong." I say from experience, "When whatever you are doing becomes so stressful that you hate getting out of the bed to go do it, you should quit doing it."

Retiring from my position as a Director in nursing at one of the larger hospitals in Memphis, was easy to do because I wanted to spend more time with my husband and live a less stressful life. In giving up a major stressor, I gained the ability to laugh and enjoy life more fully. In addition, I was able to learn to live with less income, but I experienced very minimum lifestyle changes. Leaving my job was worth the salary I gave up; however, realizing that God would provide really made it easy to retire.

The struggle comes when we try to do things in a carnal way. As born again believers, we cannot go up the ladder the way of the sinner nor the way of the carnal minded Christian. Compromising values and beliefs in order to acquire position or wealth will always prove to be a struggle between good and evil. Evil prevails when iniquity enters the heart and selfish desire is stronger than the integrity needed to do what is right. Stress and struggle go hand in hand. Both require Godly strength in order for the Christian entrepreneur to emerge as an overcomer and remain committed to exemplifying Christian principles in business.

The Bible reminds us in Psalm 127:11: *"Except the Lord build the house, they labour in vain that build it: except the Lord keep the city, the watchman waketh but in vain."* Whether building a new business or striving to rebuild a failing one, God must be allowed to direct the process and be established as the main contractor.

If you are struggling in your business it could be because you are halting between two opinions. The moment a decision is determined and the issues of "who," "what," "where," "when," and "how" are settled, the struggle will end. Ridding the body and mind of stress and struggle will yield a closer walk with the Father.

Decision making alleviates the stress and the struggle associated with indecision. God wants us to remember, as stated in II Timothy 1:7, *"For God hath not given us the spirit of fear; but of power, and of love, and of a sound mind."* We need a sound mind with which to make good, sound decisions.

Whenever there is a tug on the spirit, stop; wait; God's wisdom and subsequent instructions will be revealed as to how to proceed. The struggle of "Should I do this or not?" should be superseded by the question, "Lord, what would you have me to do in this situation?" When God's will becomes more important than financial gain and personal preference, struggle is abated, and stress is alleviated.

The act of being able to yield yourself and your business to God is really not a secret. It is a virtue. A life committed to obedience and knowing how to wait is a satisfied life and a God controlled life. When God provides the desire and knowledge to start a business, or any other project, one can be assured that He will also give strategies for success. Psalm 84:11 contains God's promise, *". . . No good thing will he withhold from them that walk uprightly."* This includes how to best do whatever it is that is being attempted. The secret to success, in any domain of your life, is often not found in modeling the steps and actions of others. In some instances, God will take you a way you know not.

One would think that seeking God's will in a Christian's life and business is easy, but it is not. Christians, if they are not very careful, find themselves modeling the actions of non-Christians in an effort to achieve fame and fortune. The Bible says, *"But thou shalt remember the Lord thy God: for it is he that giveth thee power to get wealth, . . ."* (Deuteronomy 8:18). Along with that ability, The Word of God has said in Proverbs 18:16, *"A man's gift maketh room for him, and bringeth him before great men."* As Christians, we already have within us what it takes to achieve. God has endowed us with multiple gifts and talents and the ability to excel at anything we set our hands to do. But we must do things God's way and according to His will.

Sometimes one's path to success will result in another's path to failure. I do know that "It is no secret what God will do, what He has done for others He will do for you." Trust God; release the project, person, or business to Him, and learn the secret of success without stress or struggle.

The real secret to success is becoming more like Jesus and being able to embrace and model the obedience that Jesus demonstrated in every aspect of His earthly ministry. Remember, the Israelites never had to build bricks without straw because doing so was an impossible mission for them. God sent them help, worked miracles on their behalf, and led them (all who were obedient and trusted Him) into the Promised Land.

Chapter 8

Stop the Madness

I was nearing my goal. I was building a successful team; however, the building of a network marketing team not only provided me a measure of success, increased income, and new friends, but a time of pure, sheer madness. The challenge and responsibility of training and supporting new distributors soon resulted in my engaging in unplanned and very time consuming and often impromptu drop by meetings and calls. The disruptions occurred on a daily basis, slowing me down and stopping progress. These "eaglets" demanded and received almost all of my waking hours. Telephone calls to me that just had to be answered were not uncommon as early as 5:00 a.m. and as late as 2:00 a.m.

Needless to say, my sleep cycle was continuously interrupted as a result of the constant staying up late and rising early for the early morning inquires. Usually, the answers to the questions were in the company's marketing manual or had been discussed at a previous meeting. Of course, the caller, for one reason or another, had missed the meeting and was not aware of the discussion. Many callers said that they were calling just to verify that what they had said or done was correct. Other calls were ones of sheer jubilation as distributors called to tell me of the amount of sales, number of contacts made, or potential new distributors they planned to sign up. Obviously, most of the callers had not looked at their clocks prior to calling me because they appeared surprised that I was in bed. The late hour calls seemed to be never ending, and the early morning calls (before 8:00 a.m.) became the norm for distributors who needed to talk to me before leaving for work. Before long, I began to feel drained and was often very irritable and tired. My husband, however, never complained even though he was awakened each time the telephone rang.

Within five months of starting my team I noticed a pattern of borrowing "until I can order products" was rapidly increasing. As my team grew, the borrowing of products increased. Before I could open and take inventory of my shipment, distributors would be at my office to borrow. Often they would later forget what or how much they owed me, and I would forget as well. I developed a borrow and return list to help me control the problem. As a result of the list, I was able to see that many of my downline owed me hundreds of dollars; and others a thousand dollars or more in products. Several loan lists indicated months without product return. I said to myself, "This is madness!" I knew that allowing my distributors to borrow products from me had gotten out of hand.

In addition, the distributors were not ordering enough products to service their clients. But why should they when they could borrow hundreds of dollars worth of products from me without having to return them for months?

Another serious challenge surfaced in building and stabilizing the team. Soon after opening the Inside and Out Wellness Center I noticed that in addition to counseling and promoting intake procedures for my clients, I was being sent some of my distributors' clients to perform their initial intake. Some of their reasons for sending their clients to me were,

1. No office or adequate place to see their clients
2. No scales to weigh their clients
3. No tape measure to measure their clients

One Distributor replied, "I thought you wouldn't mind since you had to do your own." These unexpected and unwanted additions to the workload caused utter chaos in my office and caused my assistant and me much distress. Of course, I quickly had to stop the infringing upon my staff and me. There were yet other occurrences that had to be discussed with the distributors:

1. calling to ask health related questions without my knowing that their clients were also on the telephone
2. coming late to meetings and leaving early
3. dropping by the wellness center at the busiest time of day and disrupting meetings with cell phones, pagers, and loud conversations
4. asking my assistant frequently to copy volumes of material at my expense for distributors to use as flyers or handouts in their meetings

65

5. not contributing to team efforts, or attending events without paying their share

Resolution came very quickly. The madness had to stop! It did not take a long time for me to realize that if I continued to allow myself, my day, and my office to be disrupted, the madness would continue.

Correcting such challenges required skillful and efficient handling. The task was to stop the chaos and encourage the appropriate behavior without causing tension and hurt feelings among the team. It was during such encounters that I thanked God most for my pastoral and professional counseling experience. Without a doubt I utilized both extensively. Corrective action was implemented, and relationships remained intact. Now, on occasion, a beeper sounds or a cellular phone rings during our meetings. But these are rare occurrences and no longer the norm.

The distributors' conduct did not change until I decided to change. The disruptions in the wellness center and in my personal business routine did not cease until I decided they must cease. The increased use of office equipment did not decrease until I discreetly suggested to each of them that they needed to purchase their own equipment or pay each time they used the equipment at the center. It was not long before requests for fax and copy assistance became rare. Distributors were also charged a small fee for training materials used as handouts at special training sessions. These charges were adequate to meet the expenses I incurred. To my surprise, no one complained.

Distributors are strongly encouraged to purchase tapes of missed training sessions and to enhance their personal and professional growth by paying to attend special seminars, such as leadership development, writing and accomplishing goals, developing purpose and mission statements, and other sessions designed to enhance their success. Professional careers are slowly being developed, and distributors are learning accountability. In order to move the team to the next level I developed a "Let Me Do It" training session to be used to get new Directors started.

Let Me Do It

L	**Learning**	Attend all team and company events. Take good notes, and review frequently. You cannot teach what you do not know. If you want to carn more, learn more.
E	**Educating**	Teach your new recruits to model networking rather than try to quickly learn to do network marketing. Teach from the company materials and the marketing manual as a means of providing accurate product and company information.
T	**Training**	Hold classes to teach your new recruits how to write mission and vision statements and to do goal setting. Hold weekly training sessions to answer questions and share knowledge you have

		gained. Use adult learning techniques and rotate responsibilities.
M	**Meetings**	Meetings must be planned, scheduled, consistent, informative, and no more than 1 ½ hours in length. Provide handouts.
E	**Empathizing**	Help new recruits overcome feelings of fear and rejection by being compassionate and understanding. Remember when you first started. Be kind, be patient, be supportive.
D	**Decision Making**	Be firm, supportive, and fair, exemplifying Christian ethics in all decision making.
O	**Organize**	Organize your office: Arrange your files and papers so they are easily found. Be coachable, and do not try to "reinvent the wheel." Recruit and build your own team. Use principles of "Retail to Enroll" in cold and warm marketing.
I	**Improve**	Strive to improve in all areas. Set goals on a monthly basis. Decrease deficiencies through self evaluation and action plans. Do weekly progress reports and tracking.
T	**Try**	Cold call, mail out yellow brochures and flyers, give out business cards, wear buttons, invite potential recruits and

customers to weekly meetings, visit web sites. If at first you don't succeed, try and try again! Never give up!

In addition, new Directors were given the following guidelines, "The Responsibilities of a New Director."

The Responsibilities of a New Director

* To have and maintain an ample supply of business aids: business cards, products, and catalogs on hand

* To learn how to track team members and numbers

* To set goals with direct upline and downline

* To hold weekly/monthly meetings with first level downline to assist with problem solving and recruitment efforts
* To be able to plan and facilitate an opportunity meeting

* To follow up on clients and new recruits weekly

* To learn qualification and maintenance guidelines for all promotional levels

* To disseminate information to downline in an accurate and timely manner

- To sponsor and/or sell on a daily basis

- To be prompt in product delivery and response to client and downline inquiries

- To attend everything and encourage downline to do the same

- To edify the organization at all times

- To exemplify excellent leadership qualities, integrity, and high moral standards

- To become a product of the product(s)

- To maintain accurate records and bookkeeping, and instruct downline to do the same

- To orient new recruits in First Fitness policy and procedures

I was able to get a grip on the situation before it spiraled downward to the point of no return: The "Let Me Do It" training session and the guidelines for Directors, along with exercising leadership, helped me to survive a near disaster. Organizational leadership is required in order to stop the madness and regain control. Even though it may have appeared that my team was being inconsiderate and overbearing, the real problem was that I had failed to recognize and take control of a bad situation at the onset.

Do not allow fear of hurting your downline's feelings cause you to experience a time of team madness. It is more difficult to recover and restore normalcy than it is to demonstrate leadership before madness evolves.

My "Blueprint" To "Success"

Chapter 9

An Eight-Strategy Blueprint for Success

Everyone, at some time or another, having undertaken new ventures, accepted new assignments, or planned a new project, has wished for a blueprint for success. Hopefully, each one of us will be able to achieve a measure of success by sheer trial and error, or better still by following in the footsteps of others who have already successfully done what we are trying to do.

Networking and building a team in multilevel marketing should come easier for those persons choosing the profession as their vehicle to success, especially since there are numerous successful people at the top of major multilevel marketing companies who are qualified and willing to serve as mentors for new distributors. I have found that having Eileen Silva for a mentor has helped me immensely in my quest to excel. She has helped me to organize, strategize, and stay goal oriented. In addition, she has shared freely with me from her wealth of knowledge. Even though she is already a Crown Presidential Director at First Fitness International, she desires my success and is encouraging me to reach the top level as well. Ascending to the very top is the dream of all new distributors who are serious about working their business.

Often, the desire to reach the top is so overwhelming and exciting that the new distributor will start his or her business without seeking wise counsel from someone who has already become successful. Taking the time to get pointers and to hear the do's and don'ts can mean the difference between success and failure. Even though there is no written blueprint for success in the network marketing business, there are strategies that can be utilized that have proven to be helpful.

I will share with you some of the strategies that I have utilized that have helped me and caused me to achieve a measure of success in a relatively short time.

Strategy I

Write the Vision and Make It Plain

The hardest thing I had to do when I started my business was to make myself sit down and write my vision, mission, and purpose statements. I have learned that if you have not written down your vision, you will not have a sense of direction, and your personal motivation will be limited. Initially, I kept saying to myself, "I don't need to write anything down because I have in my head what I want to do and how I'm going to get it done." But I soon realized that I was just making an excuse for being lazy and not wanting to "think" on paper. Actually, I have found that it is much easier and less frustrating to write down the things I want to remember than to become upset with myself because I have forgotten some previous "jewels from Jesus."

God said to Habakkuk "*. . . Write the vision, and make it plain upon tables, that he may run that readeth it. For the vision is yet for an appointed time, but at the end it shall speak, and not lie: though it tarry, wait for it; because it will surely come, it will not tarry*" (Habakkuk 2:2-3). God is speaking to us today and giving us the same words of wisdom.

If we do not get up and write down what the Holy Spirit speaks to us in the middle of the night in our dreams, before morning we will forget some, if not all, of what we were told. This is why I always keep a pad and several pens on my bedside table, easily accessible, so I can capture those precious nighttime jewels that the Holy Spirit so often gives.

God wants us to write our vision down so that when He brings it to pass we can refer to the date and time we were given the promise. It may take a while for it to happen, but it will happen. You can trust and believe if God said it to you. It will happen for you. Often, however, you will not be asleep when you see the vision. Just remember,
"Wherever God guides, He always provides."

God gives the mission and purpose after He has shown the vision. As you may already know, the purpose is most important to the vision because it is your "why." I have heard it said that if your purpose (your "why") is important enough, the mission (your "how") will be easy to accomplish. God will make the "how," your mission, easier. Remember, God's message to Habakkuk 2:2-3, quoted above. When the time is right you will know it. Changes will occur very quickly and with little or no extra effort on your part.

When we believe God, then we should not have to wait until our miracle happens to prove that what the Holy Spirit has told us is true. Instead, we should by faith act upon what we believe. For example, if the Holy Spirit has told you that you will recruit a new distributor within one month, do not wait until the month is over to start looking for the distributor; instead, begin looking immediately. When you are looking, believe that you will get the distributor by the end of the month as promised.

Making a plan is second only to writing your mission and purpose statements. When I first became a distributor, I included in my plan to achieve the position of Crown Presidential Director in First Fitness International. I planned to achieve the level within three years of joining the company. To date, I am on target within my schedule.

For quick and easy reference I keep my mission, my plan, and my purpose statements taped onto my desk, inside of the back of my personal telephone book, on the mirror in my bathroom at my home, as well as in several other places. My mission and purpose statements are my reminders. They help keep me focused and motivated. I plan my monthly recruiting efforts by writing down the names of people I expect to recruit as distributors. I do this at the beginning of each month. My projections, for personal and group volumes, are also written at the beginning of each month. (As a matter of fact, I begin planning for the next month before the last week in the current month ends.) Much of my success can be attributed to thinking my success, writing my success, and believing my success.

Writing plans and making projections are as much a part of my daily routine as getting up and going to my office. Each night, I evaluate my progress before going to sleep. You may want to call me an "on purpose person" because my "why" certainly drives me and keeps me reaching for my goals. I accomplish my goals within the times I have projected. I have not failed to meet a goal since joining First Fitness International.

I suggest if you are serious about your business that you write down your vision, mission, and purpose on tablets, as God instructed in the book of Habbakkuk. Also, develop and write your plan in the form of long term and short term goals, being careful to be clear and specific, and to include measurable and achievable time lines. Review them daily (morning and night) to keep yourself focused. Pray over them, commit them to the Lord, and then implement them. The quicker you do this the quicker you will start to see a change in your efforts.

While you are waiting for your business to grow, make sure that you are working your business to the best of your ability. *"For the vision will come; it shall not tarry."* If you can see yourself at the top and you believe that it is God's will for you to be at the top, you will get to the top! Just believe God, and do the work that it takes to get there. Write your vision, make it plain, and run with it!

Strategy II

Make Up Your Mind

If you are attempting to work in two or more companies, it is important that you make up your mind quickly as to which company is best for you. Failure is almost inevitable when a distributor tries to work three or more businesses (or network marketing companies) with equal zeal. I have seen several people successfully work two companies, but never three or more. The persons who did work the two companies successfully and simultaneously preferred one company above the other. Also, they experienced greater success in the company they favored more. I would suggest strongly that you choose only one company, and then work the one company well.

Matthew 6:24 says, *"No man can serve two masters: for either he will hate the one, and love the other; or else he will hold to the one, and despise the other. . . . "* The Scripture is very applicable to trying to give equal attention to more than one venture at a time.

I tried to continue working in my clothing business,

another network marketing business, and First Fitness. It did not take long for me to see how giving up the other two ventures would free me to put all my efforts into one business, especially since I had chosen First Fitness as my vehicle to success.

My First Fitness business took off tremendously once I made up my mind and narrowed my focus and my efforts. If you are trying to work several businesses, I suggest that you make up your mind as to which one will be the business for you. Your choice of a primary company will be your choice for achievement and success.

Strategy III

Learn What You Know You Don't Know

If you don't know what you don't know then it is imperative that you start at the beginning. Check yourself off by using your company manual, literature, tapes, and or other means that may be used for self-evaluation. Once you have determined your area(s) of deficiency, proceed immediately to correct these deficient areas.

Someone has said, "Knowledge is powerful. The more you learn, the more you will earn." The satire is, some people have the knowledge but do not use it, nor do they earn more. However, I agree that your earnings will be commensurate with your learning. It makes sense to me that you must learn your company and products in order to teach the new people who will be joining you in your business.

Matthew 15:14 says (paraphrase), *". . .Can the blind lead the blind? Shall they not both fall into the ditch?"* I, in turn, ask the question: How can you teach what you do not know? Ask your company leaders, your upline, and anyone else who may be able to help you, to provide you with the names of the best books to read, the names of leading authors, and others in the industry that are successful. Call in on weekly conference calls, use the Internet and anything else to expand your knowledge base. I have found that calling just to chat with your upline will yield more information than you can imagine. Most people are happy to help interested people learn more. Successful people usually want to be a part of helping others to become successful.

A telephone call may cost only pennies, but it can earn you millions if you ask the right questions and get the right answers from the right person. Try it! Call your upline or one of your company leaders with a question about the business. I feel certain that if they do not know the answer, they will research it and get back to you with the correct response. Do not forget to rely on the expertise of other distributors who have longevity in the company. They can also provide encouragement, support, and information. I have heard it said that "A little learning is a dangerous thing." But I say, "Not enough learning will be deadly to your career."

Strategy IV

Persistence before Pleasure

Building a team in network marketing can be like building bricks without straw, but it can be done. And it can be done a lot easier than most new distributors may think. The fear of having extreme difficulty in recruiting at the top level or maintaining a team and being able to maintain the required monthly volume sometimes scare would-be recruits away. Fear grips them before they can sign up as distributors. There are others who will try to work hard for a while, but they lack commitment and persistence. Therefore, the numbers they seek (in volume and recruitment) will not be there at the end of the month. If you have these types of experiences, do not give up! The situation will eventually change, and you will find an ace as I did when I recruited Pastors Andreá and Michael Dudley of Milwaukee, Wisconsin. I did not know how I would achieve the level of Diamond Presidential Director, but I never gave up. I did not find the Dudley's, they found me. God brought them to me just in time and when I needed them most.

Persistence has the words persist and resist scrambled within it. Both words go hand in hand for the person seeking to be successful. Whether trying to succeed in network marketing or on a conventional job, the reward will usually go to the most tenacious and persistent, hardworking, productive person. The ability to stick to a task until it is completed is meritorious. Too many people are easily distracted. Many distributors, before they know it, will find themselves involved in several ventures, and they will not be able to do well with any of them.

Persistence pays! It pays in title seeking and award efforts. In the Bible, the woman was so persistent in her pleading until the unjust judge said, *". . . Yet because this widow troubleth me, I will avenge her, lest by her continual coming she weary me"* (Luke 18:5).

So we see persistence really pays great dividends! Try being a little more persistent in your recruiting. Do not take "no" personally. Do not take "no" as a final answer. Find another way to re-approach the prospect. Never give up! Never say, "This business isn't for me." Your ace may be just around the corner. It may be the next person you could have recruited if you just had continued to work your business. Remember, the Dudley's found me; I did not find them. But I assure you I was looking, and I was expecting God to help me go to the next level. Quitting the business, if only for a little while, could cost you a million-dollar residual income later. Stay focused, be observant, expect to do well in your business, and be persistent!

Strategy V

Work, then Play; Build, then Rest

Too much of either work or play is not good. The

important thing is to temper your weeks with a lot of work and a little play throughout the week. The hardest thing for most of us to do is to stay focused. There are so many distractions to rob us of our time:

- one million telephone calls
- numerous unscheduled visitors
- drop in clients who need "just one question" answered (but they stay an hour or more)
- emergencies at home (an overhead water pipe bursts and the entire ceiling is falling)
- e-mails to respond to
- sales people
- family members who say, "We were just passing by and thought you just might want to hold your new grand baby for just a moment"
- friends who say, "I was over this way and decided to pick up a salad for both of us so we can spend a few minutes together"
- and everyday situations that only happen when you are the busiest.

The wall you are working on cannot and will not get finished if you are easily distracted.

The second hardest thing for most of us to do is play. It appears that we are cheating when we decide to take time to relax during the day or just take some needed time for self. However, when there is not enough time for play and relaxation, being under continuous stress and pressure may result in serious health problems. Our productivity will decrease, and illness will increase each time we push ourselves beyond the body's mental, physical, and spiritual capacity.

To play might mean:
- to shop
- to read an interesting, non-job related book
- to drive slowly along a different route home or just to sit quietly while taking in the scenery and feeling blessed

Some common ways to play are:
- to take small children to the park
- to listen to music
- to engage in non-competitive sports
- to go to a movie with a significant other
- to be creative with colors and crayons
- to try a new recipe, or
- to dine out with someone you enjoy

Other ways to play and relax are:
- to watch a movie
- to watercolor or paint
- to play water games
- to work crossword puzzles
- to play with a pet

There are many other special activities that may be engaged in as you learn to play and relieve the stress of the day.

I have found laughter to be the best medicine for the person with a Type A personality who is in need of relaxation and stress release. Being with babies and small children usually brings forth laughter in most people. The importance of work is not compromised when relaxation and laughter are periodically diffused throughout the work day. Deep breathing techniques as well as stretching, flexing, and tightening muscles can be done without getting up from your desk. Try some of these things I have suggested, and see how much better you will feel.

Remember, work is essential, but play is just as important. There are many domains of your life that may not be receiving the attention needed to assure that you are well balanced. Money isn't everything (even though I had a friend who once said, "It is right up next to the need for oxygen.")

God completed the work of creating earth and man, then He rested. Why shouldn't you? Working, playing, building, and resting are essential components of healthy living, and they are strategies that are often neglected. How can success be enjoyed by the over achiever that ends up exhibiting physical, mental, and spiritual illness? Failure to "unwind" and "let go" precipitates many life-threatening diseases. Every organ in the body exhibits the effects by malfunctioning or ceasing to function due to prolonged and non-alleviated stress.

In order to achieve a less stressful day, plan it, and include play and rest at appropriate intervals.

Thank You Lord

Thank you Lord—I've lived this day
It was spent in my own special way.
I laughed, I cried, and even prayed
I worked, I rested, and even played.

There were many things I meant to do
Some for me and some for you,
But now this day is at an end
A new one dawns where this has been.

Of all I've done and all I've said
I thank you for my daily bread.
I thank you Lord for allowing me
To choose my path with a will that's free.

As I close my eyes and prepare for sleep
There were many commandments I did not keep
But grace abounds for every one: I know 'tis true,
I thank you Lord—I really do!

Strategy VI

Beef up the Passion

Whenever we get excited about something, others will too. Excitement is like laughter. When a person has it and exposes it to others, they catch it and pass it on. Passion is more than desire; it is being on fire! It is being excited! It is being unable to conceal your elation! A passionate kiss sets you on fire, gets you excited, and makes it very difficult for you to conceal how you feel. Likewise, passionate distributors will ignite their prospects' curiosity and set them on fire with the desire of becoming a part of their business. The excitement that is generated will result in duplication and multiplication, and the team will grow.

How can a romance blossom from a watered down kiss? How can a powerful, productive team be produced by an unlearned and disinterested distributor? How can a class excel and enjoy a subject taught by a dry professor? And how can a team stay encouraged and upbeat without a "go getter" for a leader? Yes, these things could occur, but they would occur with difficulty and much effort. When you love what you are doing, you will find that passion is easily and naturally demonstrated.

Recruiting requires patience, knowledge, persistence, personality, and above all, passion. Given a person possesses all four of the above qualities, but lacks passion in his or her presentation and interaction, his or her recruitment efforts will not be as effective. Why? Because passion stirs excitement about the company and the products. The result is an astounding growth spurt and a tremendous pay increase. The more excited I became about what I was doing, the more my team grew, and the larger my paycheck became. The more passion I displayed in my group and one-on-one presentations, the more my team grew, and my retail sales increased. Excitement and passion generate momentum, and momentum generates income.

The ants work and work together for the good of the team. They appear to be excited as they hurry about, falling all over each other, carrying crumbs of bread. Each seems to want to be faster than the other, to fetch and carry food so everyone in the colony will eventually reap the benefits of their efforts. The Bible says in Proverbs 6:6-11, *"Go to the ant, thou sluggard; consider her ways, and be wise: Which having no guide, overseer, or ruler, provideth her meat in the summer, and gathereth her food in the harvest. How long wilt thou sleep, O sluggard, when wilt thou arise out of thy sleep? Yet a little sleep, a little slumber, a little folding of the hands to sleep: So shall thy poverty come as one that travelleth, and thy want as an armed man."*

One of my team members shared how early one morning she watched three ants carrying a worm. One ant had the front part of the worm, the second ant held the middle, and the third ant held up the rear. They marched toward their home with their prize, each ant carrying its share of the load. While on their way, the third ant lost its grip on the worm and became separated from the other two. However, the two companions continued on their journey home. The ant circled the surroundings as if it was searching for a trail that would lead to the other two ants. Each time, the ant that was lost broadened the search until the other two ants could be seen up ahead with the worm. The ant that had been carrying the latter portion of the worm passionately scrambled to regain the previously held position. As the ant reached his estranged companions, the journey continued with three ants rather than two. The returning ant was determined to share the load and continue as part of the team.

There are three lessons to be learned here:

If you desire to become successful, you must beef up the passion and go for the action. Success is not just a feeling; it is also a fact. Passion and action will cause you to reach your goals quicker than anything else I have tried.

The ability to decide when you will work, how you will work, with whom you will work, where you will work, and how much you will be paid, is most desirable. But not everyone can and/or will work productively without a boss or an overseer. The ants can. Can you? Ants appear to be happy and excited as they go about their daily task. Do you? Proverbs 6:6 says, *"Go to the ant, thou sluggard, consider her ways and be wise."* I suggest you read and re-read Proverbs 6:6-11. As you read this Scripture try to understand why the conduct and activities of the ants are important to becoming successful. Isn't it time to put a smile on your face, some pep in your step, and a little excitement in your voice? When you can inspire your team to work together, be excited, and increase their productivity, and your potential recruit becomes your new distributor, you will have learned from the ants. You will better be able to build an excited, powerful, productive, and passionate team if you possess and exemplify the basic qualities in the sixth chapter of Proverbs.

When you love what you do, others will want to do it too. I know because this is how *The Miracle Workers* team was started and why it continues to thrive. Working as a team, we are starting teams in many cities across America. Together, we are impacting health and making a difference in the lives of our downlines and our clients.

Strategy VII

Pray (without Ceasing) about Everything
(Don't Assume, Ask God)

I pray while I am walking, sitting, and even while I am talking to others. I truly try to pray without ceasing, and to pray about everything. If we did not need to do this, I do not believe the Bible would tell us to. I know that God hears and answers prayer. Therefore, I pray, then wait for God's answer (at least most of the time). Since prayer is our main source of connecting and communicating with God, and God with us, I pray on a regular basis.

I prayed an awful lot the first month after becoming a distributor with First Fitness International. Even though I prayed prior to joining the company, my prayer life became overactive after I joined. I attribute the increase in my prayer life to fear of failure, fear of the unknown, and fear of not having an upline nearby that I could confer with in a timely manner. Before I knew it, fear had gripped me and was holding me securely. I thank God for the Holy Spirit, for it was He (through prayer) that freed me from the clutches of fear.

I was told by a mother of a friend, "When fear knocks at the door, open it, and you will find that no one is there."

Someone else gave me this quote: "Fear is false evidence appearing real." I cannot remember who told me this, but I do know that it is true: prayer gets rid of fear. The Bible says, *"For God hath not given us the spirit of fear; but of power, and of love, and of a sound mind"* (II Timothy 1:7). *"And we know that all things work together for good to them that love God, to them who are the called according to his purpose"* (Romans 8:28).

In Matthew 21:22, Jesus tells us, *"And all things, whatsoever ye shall ask in prayer, believing, ye shall receive."* In addition, Jesus said, *"If ye abide in me, and my words abide in you, ye shall ask what ye will, and it shall be done unto you"* (John 15:7). With these powerful Scriptures to rely on, I always pray expecting to receive.

As modern day disciples we are heirs to the same promises because we have made Jesus our Lord. I believe in asking, believing, and receiving. When was the last time you prayed about your desires, your success, your plans, your mission, your purpose, your progress, your business, your attitude, and everything and anything that troubles you? You see, it is easy to pray without ceasing. We have so many concerns and desires. God is always waiting to hear and respond to His children. Why don't you talk to Him right now?

Here is a simple prayer that I pray often; maybe it will help you when you feel stressed and anxious in your business or overwhelmed with the possibilities of failure.

Dear Lord, I bow before you in stillness and feel you very near. Thank you for this day. Thank you for your mercy and loving-kindness.

Here are my aspirations, my hopes, and my dreams. Help me Oh God, to find Your way for me. Bless me to make Your desires for me, my desires.

I love You; I trust You; and I worship You with my whole heart. I know that You know what is best for me.

Therefore, I cast all my cares on You today; and I know that You will provide my needs. I not only pray for my business but for the businesses of others.

Thank you for the opportunity to serve. Amen.

Strategy VIII

"Share Leadership"
(Show, Tell, and Teach)

One frequent and potentially destructive mistake of many uplines is to become fearful and jealous of downline distributors who demonstrate leadership capabilities, or to be jealous of distributors who are already leaders. On the other hand, some uplines feel it is their responsibility to see that everything gets done, and gets done right. The truth of the matter is that one person cannot do it all.

The names in the story in Exodus 18:13-26, could easily

have been changed to depict the plight of many people I know that are currently in positions of leadership. Jethro, Moses' father-in-law, saw the grave error Moses was making. He told Moses (Exodus 18:17-18), *". . . The thing that thou doest is not good. Thou wilt surely wear away, both thou, and this people that is with thee: for this thing is too heavy for thee; thou art not able to perform it thyself alone."*

Jethro gave Moses a plan that would allow for division of responsibility and sharing of leadership with "able men" from within the tribe. Jethro told Moses what character and virtues to look for in the persons to be chosen as his assistants. Then Jethro told Moses (Exodus 18:22-23), *"And let them judge the people at all seasons: and it shall be, that every great matter they shall bring unto thee, but every small matter they shall judge: so shall it be easier for thyself, and they shall bear the burden with thee. If thou shalt do this thing, and God command thee so, then thou shalt be able to endure, and all this people shall also go to their place in peace."*

Keep in mind that Jethro advised Moses to share leadership and allow the "able men" to judge small matters, but to continue to judge larger matters, himself. Sharing leadership and responsibility does not mean that the leader abdicates all responsibilities. Sharing means giving away a specific part, not the entire project or assignment. Shared leadership can create team spirit, creative thinking, increased productivity, and personal pride. Not only are work and decision making shared, but also overall responsibility for team success.

Show, tell, and teach the upcoming "leaders and stars" in your downline. Do not withhold any information or training that would help them to become successful. Keep in mind that when they go up, you go up! When they are successful, you are successful! When they assist with leadership and accept responsibility, you will have fewer headaches, as well as less responsibility for the entire team's success! Your goal should be to duplicate yourself. I wish I had just three or four more Bettye Alston's. It sure would make getting to the next level much easier.

Recovery

Chapter 10

Recovery

After being called a "super mom," "super woman," and "super student," it was very difficult to think that I was not a "super network marketer." However, as I look back, I can see that even though I made numerous and often potentially devastating mistakes, I recovered. Here is my five-step plan for recovery:

1. Recovery begins with attitude.

I had a choice of one of two ways to handle my failure. I could have chosen to quit the business, never try to work network marketing again, and talk negatively about the profession to everyone I met. Or, I could do as I chose to do: cut my losses and start over. The decision I made started me toward recovery.

2. Recovery begins with forgiveness.

I had to forgive myself for the anger I felt for failing in my first three attempts in network marketing. Forgiveness must occur before healing can begin. It is just as important to forgive yourself as it is to forgive others.

3. Recovery begins with taking responsibility.

I had to take responsibility for overcharging my credit cards, take responsibility for my own success, and realize that if I was going to the top in the company and profession, it would be up to me to change the way I would work my business. In addition, I had to take responsibility for the madness that occurred in my leadership and interaction with my team. It was my responsibility to institute corrective action to subsequently stop the madness while I continued to provide support.

4. Recovery begins with change.

I had to change my leadership style, I had to change the way I worked my business, and I had to change myself to become a more dedicated, focused, and on-purpose person. To reach the pinnacle of recovery, a 360-degree change is necessary. Change is as important to success as food is to life. You must learn to see change as an ally, not as a foe.

5. Recovery begins with planning.

To plan is to succeed; if you do not plan, then you are planning to fail. Planning is difficult because it entails taking time out for thinking, visioning, writing, and disciplining yourself. Planning for your personal success comes before planning for team success.

P Pay attention	Pay attention to what is needed for you and your team.	
L Listen	Listen to your inner voice. Jesus is speaking, but you are not listening.	
A Aware	Be aware of the current market and company potential for personal growth.	
N Negotiate	Negotiate for assistance, support, and input; it will help you to design and develop your blueprint for success.	

Failure does not mean defeat. It really means an opportunity to utilize the lessons learned and experience gained, and it presents an opportunity to have a new and better beginning. Failure is a part of life. All of us will miss our goals at some point in our lives. The true failure occurs when we allow ourselves to feel defeated, accept failure, and refuse to get up and try again.

Network marketing is not for the person whose feelings are easily hurt or who takes "no" as a personal rejection. Being told "no" becomes an opportunity and a challenge for me to find a better way to present the business and the products in order to get the potential recruit or potential customer to change his or her mind and say "yes." As a result of my persistence, I have earned and enjoyed the titles of being the "top recruiter" and "top group volume winner" for two years. Obviously, I have successfully learned a little bit about how to do the business. I have learned not to hear "no." Instead, when I am told "no," I hear "maybe," "not now," or "later." Usually, the person I am talking to did not understand the business opportunity, or I did not explain the benefits of the products well. After all, who wouldn't want to lose weight, feel better, look better, and increase his or her income?

Remember, you are in a very competitive profession; you must learn to be fast paced, up to date on your product line, and have current knowledge of products and services similar to and/or in direct competition with your products and services. You must also be able to articulate with passion why your products or services are more beneficial and more desirable than others on the market. Nothing does this better than being a product of the products you are selling.

I recovered from my initial mistakes, poor leadership, and inability to build a viable team in network marketing. With hard work, perseverance, and support from excellent mentors like Shelley Baur, Eileen Silva, Taylor Hegan, and Billy and Eltha Banks, I am now a thriving network marketer. All of the mistakes I have made have been used as stepping stones to take me to the next level.

The following tips will help you to recover and/or sustain momentum and make the kind of progress you and your team deserve.

These ten basic tips are the components for full recovery and ultimate success.

Ten Success Tips

1. Keep an updated database of prospective clients and distributors. (Revise it monthly and refer to it regularly.)
2. Get the input of your distributors and your clients. They can help you by telling you what they need.
3. Have a "driving force" in place that depicts your vision, ambition, strategic plan, and short and long-term goals.
4. Provide excellent training and joint ventures with leaders in other organizations within your company. Sharing across organizational lines increases camaraderie and helps to develop team spirit. In addition, you will learn so much from each other.
5. Keep and review your historical information monthly. You should be able to see and document continuous improvement and progress each month.
6. Expect and require increased support from your more seasoned distributors. Allow them to assist you in assuming and sharing leadership.
7. Keep around you an impressive group of professionals who will make you look good, encourage you, and willingly lend their expertise to help in team development. These people are worth their weight in gold. Reward them often and publicly.
8. Recognize and reward your downline, clients, and loyal supporters publicly, promptly, and consistently. Anything that you give them is better than nothing. Often, people will work harder for praise and recognition than they will for money.

101

9. Assure a "just in time" immediate and accurate delivery system for your clients. Keep enough inventory on hand to meet the needs of your regular clients. Include a little extra for the new clients in your weekly projection.

10. Put measures in place to assure retention of your clients and downline. Retention is just as important as selling and recruiting. When you are able to retain you will discover that training time will be decreased, referrals will increase, and your income will be significantly higher each month.

Using these ten tips effectively should help to build a successful network marketing team and provide concrete guidelines for training and developing new recruits. In addition, your bank deposits will increase. Above all, I will see you at the top!

"This book of the law shall not depart out of thy mouth; but thou shalt meditate therein day and night, that thou mayest observe to do according to all that is written therein: for then thou shalt make thy way prosperous, and then shalt thou have good success"
Joshua 1:8

DEVOTIONS FOR BUSY PEOPLE
by
Rev. Dr. Neasbie Alston

✿

The Love of God

But God commendeth his love toward us, in that,
while we were yet sinners, Christ died for us.
Romans 5:8

God demonstrated His love for us when He allowed His Son to take our place on the cross. In that moment darkness covered the earth, and the voice of Jesus was heard out of the darkness saying,

"My God, my God, why hast though forsaken me?"
Matthew 27:46

God demonstrated His love by placing my sin upon Him. Since God loved us so much, how much more ought we to love God? Oh how I love Jesus because He first loved me. Amen.

❁

This Is Your Day

The spirit of the Lord God is upon me; because the Lord hath anointed me to preach good tidings unto the meek; He hath sent me to bind up the brokenhearted, to proclaim liberty to the captives, and the opening of the prison to them that are bound; To proclaim the acceptable year of the Lord, and the day of vengeance of our God; to comfort all that mourn; . . .
Isaiah 61:1-2

Today is your day to spread good news, to make some person aware of the happiness around him, to lift the spirit of the meek, to set free those that are bound by evil thoughts, evil habits, evil deeds. Today is your day to proclaim the acceptable year of the Lord because the spirit of the Lord is upon you. Then go forth into the brilliance of this day knowing that this is your day. And since this is your day, rejoice and be glad in it.

O God, let my soul rejoice in this special day that you have made for me. In the name of Jesus. Amen

❁

❀

How to Have a Healthy Mind, Body, and Soul

Let not your heart be troubled . . .
John 14:1

A troubled heart means a life filled with worry, doubt, and fear. Christian people are not supposed to be worry warts. God never intended that we should be. The emotional ties of worry and fear bring us into stress, which results in high blood pressure, heart attacks, and many other things that rob us of the true happiness of Christian freedom.

Always remember that worrying never changes anything. Instead of worrying, let us pray a prayer that someone before us has prayed.

God grant me the Serenity to accept the things
I cannot change, Courage to change the things
I can, and Wisdom to know the difference. Amen

❀

Exemplary Lives

Be ye followers of me, even as I also am of Christ.
I Corinthians 11:1

Our lives are like books that people read each day. So as they read, let them anticipate finding in the chapters of our

105

lives pure hearts, clean minds, ready hands, and willing feet. If these are found, then our lives will be filled with peace, joy, laughter, happiness, love, and serenity. When we bear these fruits of the Spirit, we will be able to say to others, "Be ye followers of me, even as I also am of Christ."

O God, give us the wisdom, the foresight, the strength and the courage to follow Thee as we bid those we lead, especially our families, to follow us. Amen.

❀

God So Loved the World

For God so loved the world, that he gave His only begotten Son, that whosoever believeth in Him should not perish, but have everlasting life.
John 3:16

Recently in a pastoral counseling class, one of the pastors told how he literally fought with his son to keep him from going the wrong way and ruining not only his life but hurting the lives of others. It is not easy to keep someone you love from going wrong. Sometimes it appears that God has to literally fight with us to keep us from going wrong.

When God finally succeeds in making us see, the end result is always success along with peace and happiness. Hopefully, you realize with the songwriter, "God loved me so, He wouldn't let go."

O God hold our hands and keep us this day
in the path of righteousness. Amen.

❀

How Are You Handling the Threats?

*Nevertheless we made our prayer unto our God,
and set a watch against them day and night,
because of them.* Nehemiah 4:9

On September 11, 2001, while America was going about
her usual way. People rose early and headed for their
workplace. All of a sudden, the peace of America was
shadowed by two planes flying into the Twin Towers of the
World Trade Center. Lives were lost; dreams were shattered,
but hope was and still is alive.

Your dreams may be shattered today, but hope has never
lost her youth. Keep hope alive and continue to follow your
dreams. The Bible teaches us to watch as well as pray.

"O God, help us this day to watch as well as pray.
For they that wait on the Lord shall renew their
strength and mount up on wings as eagles. Amen.

❀

✿

God's Protective Care

If God be for us, who can be against us?
Romans 8:31

Paul writes no other words that are more assuring to the Christian believers than these: "If God be for us, who can be against us?" God is bigger than any trouble we can be in, any problem that we must face, and He can lift any burden we must bear. He commands the wind and the waves to speak peace to the troubled mind, and He bids our "anxious fears subside." He fences me in with the Gospel of Peace in front, Songs of Joy on one side, the Oil of Love on the other side; Goodness and Mercy follow to see that I get through the valley of the shadow of death unharmed. Protected by walls like this, who shall separate us from the Love of Christ? If God be for us, who can be against us?

Father, we thank thee for allowing us to walk
each day in thy protective custody.
In the name of Jesus, we pray. Amen.

✿

Obedience to God's Commands

Children, have ye any meat? John 21:5

Peter and those who were with him had labored with

108

all their knowledge, skill and strength to catch food from the abundance of the sea in order to feed their physical bodies, only to come up with empty nets. In the morning mist, there came a voice from an outlined figure of a man standing off the shore of the sea of Tiberias saying, "Children have ye any meat?" The answer came back, "No." To this the voice replied, "Cast the net on the right side of the ship, and ye shall find." When they obeyed, they discovered that the sea willingly gave of its abundance to meet the human demands for food.

Obedience to the voice of Him who spake was the key to success for Peter and those who were with him. Obedience to that same voice can be the key to your success today. Won't you heed the master's command?

O God, open our hearts and make us receptive to thy teachings. Amen.

❀

Abiding in Christ

If ye abide in me, and my words abide in you, ye shall ask what ye will, and it shall be done unto you. John 15:7

You can have relief from your depressions, your fears, heartaches, heartbreaks, and pains of all sorts. You don't need to take Valium or tranquilizers to sleep at night. Jesus prescribes a remedy for every ill in this particular verse: If ye abide in me, and my words abide in you, ye shall ask what you will, and it shall be done unto you.

O God, help me to accept the prescribed course
that you have given for all my ills, that you
have made available to me just for the asking.
In the name of Jesus, I pray. Amen.

❁

Benediction

To Him that is able to keep you from falling and to present you before his glorious presence without fault and with great joy—to the only God our Savior be glory, majesty, power, and authority, through Jesus Christ our Lord, before all, now and forevermore! Amen. Jude 24 (NIV)

The emphasis is on the ability of Divine Authority to keep you from falling. God will keep business men and women, politicians, physicians, educators, or whatever your profession, whether skilled or unskilled. God is able to keep you from falling, and He is able to present you faultless before His presence with exceeding joy!

Accept God's promises, follow His directions, trust in Him; lean not to your own understanding, and He shall direct your path.

Oh God, give direction, and I will follow. Amen.

About the Author

●

A lifelong Memphian, Dr. Bettye J. Alston is a registered nurse and state certified professional counselor and holds M. Div., D. Min, and Ph.D. degrees. She is an energetic, sixty-two-year-old, great-grandmother with a purpose, though a late comer to network marketing. Her fifteen years as a state certified counselor, and thirty-two years as a nurse have prepared her for a ministry that encompasses health and wellness.

Dr. Alston, a pastor for twenty-four years, is founding pastor of New Beginning Ministries Church of Our Lord and Saviour Jesus Christ, located in Memphis, Tennessee. She opened the Inside and Out Wellness Center in Memphis in April 2000, after she learned about the healing, anti-aging, and restorative benefits of natural products, herbs, and dietary supplements. She discovered that her body was better able to combat fatigue, stop the accumulation of fat, and decrease health challenges with the use of natural products, proper diet, exercise, and pure water. Her personal success and the success of her wellness center have compelled her to seek to help other pastors with their health challenges and to have them start wellness centers within their churches.

In August 1999, Dr. Alston joined First Fitness International, a network marketing company that specializes in weight loss and wellness products. She quickly earned the title of Diamond Presidential Director and is well on her way to achieving the top position of Crown Presidential Director. Her team, *The Miracle Workers*, has rapidly and steadily grown as monthly sales indicate momentum. With little effort, she and her team have consistently exceeded their previous months' sales volumes. As a result, she achieved first place trophies and recognition in 2000 and 2001 for recruitment and group volume. In addition, she has been awarded five star dream vacations to such places as Ireland, Hawaii, the Bahamas, and is in the process of winning a trip to South Africa in March 2002.

Dr. Alston is currently enrolled in the Clayton College of Natural Health in Birmingham, Alabama, where she is pursuing a course of study as a Doctor of Naturopathy in order to better serve her clients at the Inside and Out Wellness Center. Dr. Alston states, "I have come full circle, know my mission and purpose, and am now able to use my education and God-given gifts to help people *really* get well.

Dr. Alston is married to Rev. Dr. Neasbie Alston, who is a successful Baptist pastor of forty-nine years. They are the parents of eight, the grand parents of eighteen, and the great-grand parents of eight.

Both Dr. Bettye Alston and Rev. Dr. Neasbie Alston are "products of the products" they sell and have achieved tremendous weight loss success. They enjoy helping their organization achieve health and wealth as they build successful businesses and establish wellness centers across America. When asked the question, "Is there anything too hard for you to do?" Dr. Alston's response is a resounding "No." One of her favorite Scriptures is found in Philippians 4:13: *"I can do all things through Christ which strengthens me."*

❁